WHAT WOULD GEORGE DO?

WHAT WOULD GEORGE DO?

Advice from Our Founding Father

NAN MARSHALL AND HELEN BRODER

PELICAN PUBLISHING COMPANY

Gretna 2013

The word "Pelican" and the depiction of a pelican are
trademarks of Pelican Publishing Company, Inc., and are
registered in the U.S. Patent and Trademark Office.

Library of Congress Cataloging-in-Publication Data

Marshall, Nan, 1945-
What would George do? : advice from our founding father/ by Nan
Marshall and Helen Broder.
    pages cm
Includes bibliographical references.
ISBN 978-1-4556-1859-0 (pbk. : alk. paper)—ISBN 978-1-4556-1860-6
(eBook)
    1.   United States—Social life and customs—21st century. 2.
Washington, George, 1732-1799—Influence. 3.   Etiquette—United
States—History—21st century. 4.   Conduct of life—United States—
History—21st century. 5.   Washington, George, 1732-1799. Rules of
civility. 6.   United States—Social life and customs—18th century. 7.
Etiquette—United States—History—18th century. 8. Conduct of life—
United States—History—18th century. I. Broder, Helen. II. Title.
    E161.M335 2013
    973.92—dc23
                          2013036414

Printed in the United States of America
Published by Pelican Publishing Company, Inc.
1000 Burmaster Street, Gretna, Louisiana 70053

For our husbands, Gene and Jim

Contents

"First in war, first in peace, and first in the hearts of his countrymen."

—Henry Lee's eulogy of George Washington, 1799

Introduction

When we decided to write a book about good behavior and its long-standing place in the American psyche, we went looking for a place where history and etiquette intersected. We found it in the 110 *Rules of Civility & Decent Behaviour in Company and Conversation* or *Rules of Civility* as they are commonly called. These are precepts of refinement compiled by French Jesuits in 1590 and translated into English by Francis Hawkins in London around 1640. Like many students in his day, George Washington copied out and memorized these social rules and morals in an effort to learn how to conduct himself in the fashion of a proper eighteenth-century Virginia gentleman. History stands as a testament that he learned his lessons well. The Founding Father of our nation was also the Founding Father of American manners. As a successful gentleman farmer, courageous general, and diplomatic statesman, Washington impressed his character and style on the entire country.

Washington's *Rules of Civility* ring as true in today's accelerated social environment as they did centuries ago. Civility is both our birthright and our responsibility, and all of us, with a little practice and mindfulness, can become considerate, civil, socially at-ease Americans who would make the Father of Our Country proud.

I live in Savannah, Georgia, a town noted for its graciousness and hospitality. Yet I found myself profoundly moved when, less than a year after 9/11, I visited a friend's Lower Manhattan apartment and discovered a palpably transformed, gallant New York. A wave of courtesy had swept the city. The atmosphere of hurried self-absorption I remembered from past trips had been replaced with one of warmth and genuine solicitousness toward one another. It struck me that New Yorkers had faced their tragedy by reconnecting with their humanity. It made me realize this is the real America, a land not only of the brave but also of generous, compassionate people.

Why, I wondered, is this compassionate side of Americans not more often celebrated or cherished in everyday practice? Instead of generating continual reports of unbecoming conduct at rock concerts, on tennis courts, and even in hallowed halls of government, why can't we appreciate and propagate more acts of kindness and goodwill? Surely refined, considerate, dignified behavior could be practiced without waiting for tragedy to call it into being.

That is how I began my reflections on timeless manners in a changing society. I set out to consider good American manners not as a mere "decoration," but as an expression of our identity. The rules that my daughter Helen and I examine here are intended as tools for making connections with other people and for making ourselves and our community whole.

Because of the vagaries of my life, there has seldom been a time when I haven't had to ponder the dos and don'ts of proper manners. After a lifetime of this, I have learned that whether you are the new neighbor, the new employee, or even the new spouse, adherence to George Washington's codes of behavior will ease transitions, smooth awkward situations, and soften the edges of rough times.

I do not recall at what point I first became aware that something was odd about my manners. Perhaps it occurred when I was constantly reprimanded at school for my failure to say "Yes, ma'am," or "Yes, sir." I had been taught how to speak properly, all right. In my family, it was considered bad manners to speak substandard English—to dangle a participle was horribly rude. However, because my parents abhorred anything that suggested servility, "ma'am" and "sir" were not part of my vocabulary.

Growing up in the South without practicing these respectful responses made life difficult for a little girl who wanted to be accepted.

As my life began to unfold through its bumps, twists, and turns, I was baffled. Something was missing from the instruction of my youth. I tried to sift through the mixed and often quirky messages I had received from my parents in order to understand what was good and not so good about my behavior. I recognized and appreciated the values my parents had tried so hard to instill in me, yet I knew there were glaring gaps. What to keep? What to let go? I needed to find some basis for knowing how to act. What was style? What constituted hospitality? Where was the give and take of good conversation? Were laughter and silliness allowed? How did one make and keep friends?

I examined myself and cringed as I listed my shortcomings— those failed introductions, less than stellar table manners, my proclivity for tardiness, unreturned phone calls, and on and on. I ruminated over my small acts of benevolence gone awry and my well-meant yet misinterpreted words.

I must confess, I was also quick to recall the foibles of others. There was the overnight guest who complained that the water pressure was insufficient for a good shower. I'll never forget my mortification when a dinner companion lambasted the waiter about the sauce on her steak. Or what about the man whose zingers left me humiliated and speechless? At one point during the research for this project, my husband Gene, tired of my belaboring all manner of infraction, humorously suggested I retitle the book, "Everything Ever Done to Annoy."

I discovered that in the stepped-up pace of the twenty-first century—the madness of our schedules and the rushing to stay ahead—we often forget the common courtesies that are intrinsic to our American heritage. This book is meant to be a reminder to refocus on the things that make our society great: generosity, bravery, kindness, honesty, loyalty, and consideration. I have tried to make a passionate cry for civility yet not to rant and rave about our shortcomings. After all, as our first president so aptly puts it in Rule 48, *Wherein you reprove Another, be unblameable yourself; for example is more prevalent than Precepts.*

Nan Marshall
August 2013

My first inkling of the need to put together a book of practical advice about how to behave in an ever-changing America coincided with the birth of my twins, Bill and Charlie. Amidst the incredible euphoria, my husband Jim and I (like all new parents) found ourselves asking some daunting questions. What is the foremost thing we want for them? What does it mean to live a good life? Do we want them to be well-liked? Are we primarily concerned that they be good citizens? Is financial success important? How about the noble concept of making the world a better place?

It dawned on me that if our children were to forge a path in life, they would need to make sense of the competing perspectives and agendas of an increasingly complex world. Education was valuable. Money would help, of course—my children would figure that out soon enough. But slowly I began to acknowledge that the most significant advantage I could give them would be the cultural capital of knowing how to get along well with others. Superior social skills would make them more likable and respected. If they knew what to do and when to do it, they would feel comfortable and put others at ease. When opportunities opened, they would be prepared to connect successfully with others in our diverse society.

Thank goodness motherhood is no longer the first job most women tackle! We learn so much in our first jobs, and we need that preparation for parenting. For my first job, I entered the field of sports marketing. I loved working with Olympians, people who had plugged away in anonymity, not with the expectation of making millions of dollars in professional sports but for the pure love of the sport. What I learned from them is that true sportsmanship—with its emphasis on courage, rigorous discipline, and a sense of fair play—is a blueprint for character development and civilized deportment.

In searching for more clues as to what constitutes modern manners, I invariably turned back to the long-valued ways of proper behavior in my family, whose roots go back to colonial Georgia. I found the women especially important. These stylish, sparkling women, prepared from birth to possess all the graces, served as inspirations to a distant relative of mine, the best-selling novelist Ferrol Sams. Mixing humor and old-fashioned moralizing, his fiction sprang from family history. Elegance, according to Ferrol, originates in the realm of the "Hodnett." For him, "Hodnett" is a synonym for a "quality lady raised properly." Knowing that my great-grandmother was a "Hodnett," he explained further, "You learn your manners, your culture, and your diction at your mother's knee."

But where can youth look for shining character models in twenty-first-century America? Gone are the days when primers blended moral lessons with history and legends of Washington's integrity were standard fare. Why do family, church, and school no longer instruct and impose the rules of social order? Today, with no authority in place and conflicting ideas of what to believe, it is no surprise that civility is on a rapid downhill slide. As I began expanding and updating the *Rules of Civility*, I realized that the changing patterns of contemporary society make it even more difficult to know how to act. A sense of entitlement is often confused with self-esteem. Authentic speech and actions seem increasingly rare. Questionable business ethics and Darwinian survival tactics are on the rise. With all the changes transforming our world, I continue to believe in the value of considerate behavior as the vibrant element that—if learned and practiced properly—will fortify my children as they navigate the challenges of modern life.

Associate yourself with Men of good quality if you Esteem your own reputation; for 'tis better to be alone than in bad Company, Washington advised in Rule 56. The most important thing that we can do is make sure that we are of good quality and can recognize the same in the people we attract. Popularity is fleeting; rather than striving to become the person everyone likes, it is better to be the person everyone wants to befriend. It is when we genuinely crave the high regard of someone that we value their company.

Helen Broder
August 2013

CHAPTER ONE

Making Time

If George Washington had been able to step into a time machine 250 years ago for a journey forward to the twenty-first century, what would he think of the tempo of our lives? The dizzying demands that intrude on modern life at breakneck speed, and with apparent boundlessness, test both our physical limits and our cognitive range. Our packed days are time-pressed; our hours are precious. There is nothing especially wrong with this, but it does tend to take a toll on courtesy. For some, being busy has become an excuse to be rude or, at best, less than gracious. There's no such thing as civility on the fly.

Today's chock-a-block lifestyle demands that we juggle, at a minimum, two or three things every single minute. Can we rise above the fray? Can we take a break from the frenetic schedule set by long work hours and pervasive electronics? Can we afford the time to consider the welfare of others over the short-term needs of self?

Staying calm, assuming good faith, and remaining civil is not (and should not be) a revolutionary idea. The *Rules of Civility* shaped our Founding Father's character and taught him to make a habit of slowing down, listening to, and looking out for the other person. Washington's life was not always easy: he endured a string of defeats in his personal, military, and political life; but he confronted the setbacks with the faith that he could achieve what he had set forth to do. As our leader philosophically reflected, "Human affairs are always checkered and vicissitudes in this life are rather to be expected than wondered at."[1] History stands as a testament to his success over adversity. Can we follow in the footsteps of the resolute and ever-courteous George Washington? Yes, we can. At the start of each subsequent chapter, as well as scattered throughout the text, you will find sage advice from our first president, with further advice on how to apply it to modern life.

KNOWING WHY WE RUSH

Most people, if asked, say they would prefer a balanced and relaxed approach to life. Why, then, do they so often adopt a harried lifestyle, even though it does not make them more productive? Because they have become addicted to stress.

Stress addiction can take many forms. *Schedule junkies* get a burst of adrenaline from feeling rushed. By constantly adding false items to their list of necessities, they feed their need to be busy, feel busy, and look busy. Many of us share this addiction. Busyness—multitasking, having a full calendar, being double-booked, stretching ourselves thin, being forever on the run—has become a prerequisite for our feeling good about ourselves.

The *information junkie* is a technology addict who needs to know everything that is happening at every moment. Hooked up to a twenty-four-hour-a-day news grind with his smartphone, computer, iPad, Kindle, and GPS, he is unable to power down. For fear of what he might be missing, he misses the best thing life offers—a connection with others.

The *self-important* person creates a "to do" list that he cannot possibly complete but refuses to alter. He inflates his sense of importance by inflating his workload. Confusing productivity with mere activity, this basket case moves too fast to realize how much he is distressing others.

The *guilty* person has a free-floating sense of guilt associated with leisure. He has bought into the Puritan work ethic in a major way and keeps himself busy so that no one will think him lazy or useless. Not only does he fail to help anyone else, but also his constant make-work projects cause an irony: he becomes more useless after all.

The *frightened* person stays busy so that he does not have to face his fears. A good prescription for depression is to plan active days, but these unhappy souls often become like hamsters on a wheel. Ironically, the most important factor associated with happiness and well-being—meaningful relationships with other human beings—continues to elude these lonely folk as they run themselves ragged.

The *confused* person keeps scurrying to and fro like a rat in a maze, hoping that he will find his way. As Yogi Berra quipped, "I don't know where we're going, but we're making great time!" When something important happens, this person does not respond appropriately, because he does not know how. Bumbling through life, he is not purposely inconsiderate, yet he simply is.

The *pathetic* person is constantly involved in a crisis and thinks that because of his pitiful state he is exempt from all expressions of common courtesy. How can he be expected to sympathize with other people when he is barely escaping some catastrophe?

One common, modern way of dealing with these stress addictions is no better than the addictions themselves. Consider the *reluctant* person. The popular self-help advice of saying "No" as a way to avoid stress has created a group of people who avoid committing themselves to *anything*. These people make saying "No" even to friends in need feel natural.

We all need to slow down. Busyness is a poor substitute for genuine living, and it doesn't fool anyone. Worst of all, it isolates the people who hide behind it from a positive connection with life and other people. Life is full of things one simply cannot drop, but if you are busy from morning till night like most people, with a hundred places to go and things to do, do not despair. Ask yourself what has to be done no matter what, what can wait, and what can be delegated.

As a French businessman noted, "No one ever appreciated better than George Washington the value of time and the art of making use of it."[2] He never appeared to be in a hurry. Despite the hustle and bustle of war, politics, and farming, he always maintained an elegant air of comfortable ease.

It is not some great show of busyness, but the tasks we actually accomplish, that make us look impressive. Still, it can be hard to let go of the show. If you need to start by focusing on how your attitude appears, then appear relaxed and carefree, as if you have time to stop and listen to others. Do not worry if you do not feel it yet. By appearing relaxed and carefree, you not only make other people feel welcome and valuable, but you also radiate the message, "Of course I don't look busy. I did it right the first time."

Final Thoughts

Contemporary life has not made us uniquely harried. The relentless passage of time has always existed—the ticking clock, the hourglass, the sundial, or the setting sun itself. Although we'd like to think that time pressure was invented about the same time as the digital clock, the truth of the matter is that time-management challenges have been around forever. Fortunately, so has the cure—social contact.

As George Washington reminded us, sharing time with a friend has always been, and will always be, a choice. Detained in Philadelphia and desperately trying to raise the money to pay his army, Washington missed the fellowship of his officers away on the southern campaign. He wrote General Greene, "To participate and divide our feelings, hopes, fears and expectations with a friend is almost the only source of pleasure and consolation left us in the present and uncompromising state of our affairs."[3]

The same minute can be given resentfully or gladly. The art is not merely making time, but making time gracefully. Attempt to eliminate the expression "I have to," and instead use the terms "I get to," "I want to," or "I choose to." The more we anchor our awareness on the "here and now" and the more we embrace the moment, the better use we can make of what precious time there is.

CHAPTER TWO

The Social American

Every Action done in Company, ought to be with Some Sign of Respect to those that are present.

—Rule 1

Colonial social life revolved around fancy balls and assemblies, the theater, fox hunting, and the racetrack. Pioneers gathered for barn raisings, picnics, square dances, and prayer. In modern times, we need look no further than Labor Day, Memorial Day, Presidents Day, Flag Day, the Fourth of July, and Veterans Day (and maybe even the Super Bowl) to fill our social calendars. We thrive on human contact.

But only a lucky few are completely at ease in the company of other people. For most of us, socializing takes some effort. The introverts among us may shrink from socializing altogether, neither giving nor attending parties, because they are overwhelmed with uncertainties that cause them to feel dull, self-conscious, and anxious. As a result, they believe that they cannot entertain at the proper level and have nothing to say. In actuality, staying at home because of imagined inadequacies feeds fear and makes it harder to go out the next time.

The extrovert may do the opposite: entertain a great deal, attend many parties, join everything, and go to great lengths to see and be seen. Not everyone who leads such an apparently enviable life is happy. Riding a social whirlwind to the "right" places, wearing the "right" clothes, and schmoozing only the "right" people does not guarantee any genuine connectedness and ultimately can leave the extrovert feeling cold, empty, and more than a little desperate.

Wherever you fall on the social comfort scale—gadfly or wallflower—the key to every social situation is to be positive, warm, and sincerely curious about the people you encounter. Successfully exuding genuine interest will make everyone around you feel comfortable. A certain lightness prevails when the spotlight shifts from center stage (self) to full theater (others).

Reaching Out

Although some societies greet friends with a kiss and less intimate associates with a bow, Americans have no set protocol. Some people hug everybody in the room; others keep a formal distance. As a result, the nuances of the ordinary greeting become a complicated social vernacular. Not only do we have to know whether to shake hands, hug, or kiss, but also how to do so.

Could George Washington be elected today? Our first president was not a politician who excelled in "pressing the flesh." At receptions, he stood with one hand resting on his sword and the other holding a tri-cornered hat, and he greeted his constituents with a formal bow. Perhaps unfortunately, this particular greeting method will not work for us. Not many people today even own a sword or a tri-cornered hat, much less know how to use them in a social context. It seems George cannot help us with specific advice in this area.

However, remember Rule 1: *Every Action done in Company, ought to be with Some Sign of Respect to those that are present.* A handshake conveys a demonstration of good will and is intended to communicate sincerity, strength, and professionalism. Its proper execution is critical to its success. A good handshake is firm but not viselike (please don't hurt me!). A bad handshake is limp and can be interpreted as a sign of weakness or lack of confidence. A snobby handshake presents only the tips of fingers. If the handshake is performed well but lacks eye contact, the well-meaning gesture becomes meaningless.

Keeping up with the language of social hugs can be harder than keeping up with the Adams. Social hugs are complex, because they convey different levels of familiarity and are constantly evolving in form. You have the one-handed hug, the "good friend" back pat or shoulder squeeze hug, the full frontal "you're really special" hug, and the intimate hug with back rub. Be sure to use the one most appropriate to the relationship and the culture. And remember, he who initiates the hug also concludes the hug.

Social kisses also come in many forms. The old-fashioned hand kiss, in which the gentleman cradles the lady's hand, raises the hand to chest-level, and bends to kiss or almost kiss the hand with his lips, has been replaced by the cheek kiss. The cheek/air kiss can be initiated by both men and women and is used to say "hello" or "goodbye." Both parties lean forward, offer a right cheek, and purse lips. Actually brushing cheeks or making a discreet "mwah" sound is optional. The one-cheek kiss has in recent years been replaced by the two-cheek kiss. The sophisticated double-kiss is warm and fun but can be complicated, for it often results in rather comical nose bumping or unintentional lip smacking.

After a warm initial greeting, arm's length intimacy will suffice. Respect personal space, the region surrounding one's body that one feels is private. An obvious clue that you are intruding occurs when you step forward and the other party steps back. If you are a touchy-feely personality type, learn to keep a respectful distance from others by imagining that you have a hula hoop around you. Heed Rule 37: *In Speaking to men of Quality do not lean nor Look them full in the face, nor approach too near them at le(a)st Keep a full Pace from them.*

Are you someone who constantly doles out hugs, shoulder rubs, or high fives? Do you find yourself grabbing people by the arm or tapping them to get their attention? Some people love this physical contact; others hate it. Because touch is subjective, until you can figure out when yours is welcome, it is best to keep your hands to yourself.

It might seem motherly to fix the personal attire of others, but do your acquaintances really want you to be their mother? If someone has missed a belt loop or has a collar turned in, a label showing, lint on the shoulder, a shoe untied, or buttons misaligned, let it be. It is not your job to groom the world. You might think you are being helpful, but your friend is likely to find it disconcerting, invasive, or condescending. Remember what George says in Rule 70: *Reprehend not the imperfections of others for that belongs to Parents, Masters and Superiors.* With that said, if anyone is in a situation that would provoke great embarrassment—pants unzipped or spinach stuck between teeth—it is appropriate to quietly make him or her aware of the problem.

Meeting and Greeting

Respect begins with acknowledgement. As George Washington reminds us in Rule 28, *If any one come to speak to you while you are Sitting Stand up.* Greet everyone in the crowd and make an effort to include everyone in the conversation. If you pass someone you recognize, say, "Hello," even if you believe that he or she may not remember you. No one ever minds a friendly greeting. Everyone deserves a smile. Snubs, whether intentional or careless, always hurt.

Learn people's names. Possessing an excellent memory for names, Washington seldom required a second introduction. When introduced, look at the person and repeat the name back to him or her: "Hello, Charlie, it's nice to meet you." To address someone as "girlfriend," "buddy," "sweetie," "honey," "dear," or "sugar" usually indicates that you have not bothered to remember his or her name. Such monikers are best reserved as terms of endearment for an intimate friend or family member.

It is not a crime to forget a person's name; the crime is forgetting the person. When you are on the spot, remember that others may have the same problem you do. If you are not sure you have met someone, saying your own name in greeting will often prompt him or her to give a name in return. If you can, add another sentence to let the individual know you recognize him or her. For example, you could say, "Hi, I'm Dolly Madison. I met you at Abigail's birthday." If you forget names while making an introduction, do not apologize. Say, "Have we met before?" and most likely they will take the cue and introduce themselves. When you are introduced to someone that you think you *may* have met before, do not say, "Glad to meet you." The person will realize that you do not remember him. It is safer to say, "Glad to see you."

If you are huddled in a group and another person approaches, move back to open up the circle and let the newcomer feel welcome to join the conversation. As George puts it in Rule 8, *At Play or at Fire, its Good manners to Give Place to the Last Comer.* Introduce people and try to find a common thread of connection—schools, hobbies, neighborhoods—that will stimulate conversation.

Rule 75, *If you Perceive any Stop because of your coming you may well intreat him gently to Proceed,* reminds the newcomer to a group to avoid interrupting the ongoing conversation. If you have something to say on a totally different subject, wait for a natural shift. If you want to speak to one person privately, wait for the group to disperse.

Cliquishness occurs when two or more people say or do something that excludes others—talking across others in whispers, speaking a foreign language the others do not understand, or sharing inside jokes. George addresses this when he reminds us in Rule 77, *Whisper not in the Company of Others.* Less obvious but equally painful to the outsider is any discussion of invitations to past or future social events from which he or she may have been or will be excluded. Similarly, never make an invitation to only one person if there are others present. Either invite everyone or wait to ask privately later.

PARTY TIME

THE HOST WITH THE MOST

Throwing a party is a way of expressing your friendliness and desire to entertain others. When you invite someone to be your guest, you are conveying the message, "I enjoy your company and want to entertain you." A good host has a talent for making everyone feel comfortable and appreciated. So reach out and set your guests at ease with kindness and thoughtfulness.

Anticipate their preferences. Remember, the party is not about you; it is about your desire to bring pleasure to others.

On Election Day, July 24, 1758, the "committee to elect George Washington" entertained prospective voters with copious beverages—thirty-four gallons of wine, three pints of brandy, thirteen gallons of beer, eight quarts of cider, and forty gallons of wine punch. In a note to his campaigners, the absentee candidate Washington worried, "My only fear is you spent with too sparing a hand."[1]

When you feel and think outside yourself, your ability to entertain will improve. You might like to play games that are of no interest to others. You might like to sit in the sun, while others might like to sit in the shade. You might not be hungry, while others crave a snack. This list could go on endlessly. Rather than assuming that others share your likes or dislikes and forcing specific foods or activities on them, provide a few options.

It is important to be very clear about the nature of the event when issuing the invitation. "Happy Birthday" does not mean you can plan a party for yourself and ask the guests to pay the bill. Likewise, home-show parties are a business and, fun as they might be, do not surprise guests with the unexpected selling of clothes, jewelry, cleaning supplies, and makeup. Even if you are planning a charitable fundraiser, it is not fair to lure unwary participants. No one wants to be caught off guard, especially when it involves money.

THE GOOD PARTY GUEST

If you want an active social life, follow a few simple courtesies, and you stand a better chance of being invited a second time. Let the host know if you are coming, and do not assume that your pet and/or friend are implicitly welcome. For reasons of space and perhaps cost, the host probably has had to exclude some people that he would have liked to invite. You may inform your host that you regretfully cannot attend because you have a guest, date, or cannot leave your dog. At that point, the host has an opening to choose to invite your companions or not.

Punctuality was one of Washington's strong points, and he expected his guests to be on time. If guests were tardy by even five minutes for an official presidential dinner, Washington would already be seated and would testily explain that the cook was governed by the clock and not the company.[2] His receptions were held at three o'clock. At three-fifteen, the doors were shut to further visitors.[3]

With this in mind, remember an invitation to dinner means "come within twenty minutes" of the agreed upon hour. If a party is set for six o'clock to eight o'clock, come by seven o'clock at the latest. It is frivolous to flit in at the last minute.

On the other hand, arriving at a party early is just as rude as coming extremely late. A good host may make entertaining seem effortlessly gracious, but even the pros are prone to last-minute preparations and confusion. Walk around the block if you have to, but *never* show up early.

A party pooper goes home too soon. If you must leave before the end, alert the host in advance. You may express your regret at having to leave earlier than you would like; but if your departure is triggered by having another party to attend, do not mention it. It is an insult to suggest you have squeezed the event into your busy schedule. Depart without fanfare so that the other guests will not prematurely follow you out the door.

The mark of a successful party is that people hate to see it end, and it is the rare host who is not flattered to find people lingering. But there are limits and exceptions, and the good guest knows when to go home. Be alert to signals telling guests it is time to leave. Has the music been turned off? Is the host standing and angling toward the door? An obvious clue is that most of the other guests have already left. Try not to be the first or the last to go. Aim for somewhere in the middle.

The Houseguest

Have you ever wondered why "George Washington slept here" is such a common claim to fame among colonial-era homes? Riding a horse from place to place with inns few and far between, young Washington had to depend on friends and friends of friends for a warm bed during his travels. At age sixteen, on a surveying trip in the Blue Ridge Mountains, he wrote, "I found nothing but a little straw matted together, without sheets or anything else, but only one threadbare blanket, with double its weight of vermin, such as lice, fleas etc."[4] Later, of course, he fared considerably better, as was his due. Seeking well-appointed houses, young George quickly adapted to the second part of Rule 32: *To one that is your equal, or not much inferior, you are to give the chief Place in your Lodging, and he to whom 'tis offered ought at first to refuse it but at the Second to accept though not without acknowledging his own unworthiness.* He accepted the best from his host (albeit with a slight show of false modesty). We may do likewise, as long as we realize that there may be limitations on what the host is *able* to offer.

When Washington became famous, he found himself forced to keep an open house at Mount Vernon. Although a domestic wing was added in 1773-74, the house remained crowded. In the seven years between 1768 and 1775, about two thousand guests visited Mount Vernon.[5] This stream of visitors ranged from relatives and intimate friends to travelers in need of lodging for the night. It was not uncommon for three to five visitors to share a room.[6] Even if you had the privilege of being a guest at Mount Vernon, it would have been up to you to adjust your habits to those of the house, not vice versa.

When you are a guest, leave your white glove at the door. Do not find fault in the household arrangements or point out shortcomings in the housekeeping. The presence of a bug or the expiration date on the groceries is best left unmentioned.

A good guest tries to figure out the household idiosyncrasies. When invited to share the intimacy of someone's home overnight, pay attention. Is the bathroom door left open, shut, or cracked? Are toilets flushed during the night? Which items are recyclable—glass, aluminum, or paper? Do certain lights customarily stay on or off?

Unless your host sets the precedent, do not even think about smoking in the house. In a non-smoking home, the odor of stale cigarettes will linger long after you have left. If you must smoke, go outside and take pains to leave no evidence of your habit.

Not everything in a private home is guest friendly. Even if your host has told you to "make yourself at home," do not abuse his goodwill by putting your feet on the coffee table, flipping television channels, taking a nap on the couch, or snooping behind shut doors, in drawers, or in closets.

Does George Washington have anything to say about prying eyes? You bet he does. Whenever you are around your host's papers, remember the admonishment of Rule 18: *Come not near the Books or Writings of Another so as to read them unless desired or give your opinion of them unask'd, also look not nigh when another is writing a Letter.* This applies to computers as well; so never use someone's computer without permission. Even with permission, take care to leave no signs of your activity, such as downloading anything or rearranging the icons on the desktop.

Treat your host's property with respect and care—more care, really, than you exercise in your own home. Tracking dirt into the home, putting wet drinking glasses on wooden surfaces, scattering cheese Crunch'ems on the couch, and heaving your full weight onto a fragile bench all risk giving your host cleaning or repair headaches after your departure.

In short, a good overnight guest tries to fit imperceptibly into another's house. This applies especially in the bedroom and bathroom. In the bathroom, rinse and dry the tub, sink, and toilet carefully after use—*each* use if the bathroom is shared. Leave the bed made in the same fashion in which you found it. Offer to strip the sheets, and if you do, remake the bed with clean sheets or at least the top covers.

One universal rule will help ensure you are welcomed back often: make your visits reasonably short. Benjamin Franklin, the all-American dispenser of good advice, said that houseguests, like fish, begin to smell after three days. No matter how amusing and polite you are, you can always overstay your welcome.

FINAL THOUGHTS

We are social creatures. There are many reasons to strike up an acquaintance; most obviously, you might make a friend or learn something useful. So why, if we enjoy interacting face to face, have we let the chaos of television, video games, cell phones, and text messaging dominate our free time? We need to turn back to the real world, unplug, step outside, and visit with friends. Do not wait for a power outage or loss of your Wi-Fi signal to force you to disconnect from your high-tech paraphernalia and reconnect with face to face relationships. Rediscover the joy of eye contact and the energy of good conversation. Revel in shared laughter. If you do, you will discover how you fit with people, how people fit with you, and how you fit with the world.

CHAPTER THREE

Keep In Touch

*Be not forward but friendly and Courteous; the first to Salute hear
and answer & be not Pensive when it's a time to converse.*

—Rule 66

"Let's promise to keep in touch," are so often the parting
words of friends, family, and associates. Paradoxically, in an age
that is daily more interactive, it is getting harder and harder to
make good on that promise. In a world on the move and in a
time of revolutionary communication technologies, we seem
increasingly challenged to connect with gentleness and caring
and with grace notes of the spoken or written language. Hyper-
connected, we participate in the exchange of information rather
than in an exchange of humanity. As the most wired people in

history, we seem to have lost our emotional connections. Without consideration or courtesy, we barrage our correspondents with blogs, newsletters, forwarded jokes, and unedited masses of pictures. We broadcast run-on, stream-of-consciousness missives to "groups" of friends. Words spill out of us willy-nilly, not always with sufficient regard to their consequences or the feelings of those who will be reading or hearing them.

Keeping in touch is equal parts pleasure and duty, whether one is using a quill pen or a tweet. George took his correspondence very seriously and believed every letter deserved a courteous answer. "I will retire to my writing table and acknowledge the letters I have received."[1]

CORRESPONDENCE

If you have ever come across one of your old letters, you have probably been fascinated by how vividly it captured a moment in your life. Whether it was a message home from summer camp, a postcard from the beach, a profession of love, an angry tirade, or even a gracious thank-you, it preserved a piece of you. In their indelible nature, written or recorded words are often the clues we leave behind that reveal who we were and what kinds of things occupied our lives. These records of joy, hope, opinion, and regret remain a voice for posterity long after your voice is gone.

Washington understood well the power his personal papers would have over his future reputation. Instead of storing his rough original drafts, he wanted clerks who wrote with a "fair hand"[2] to produce a magnificent set of bound papers. His trove of wartime correspondence filled twenty-eight volumes.[3]

Be it quill or tweet, do not be derailed by carelessness in your correspondence. Proofread your letters. Common errors are especially glaring when seen in print. After all, 280 years later, you are probably wincing at the random capitalization and odd spellings Washington used in copying his *Rules of Civility*. (If so, remember that this was the work of a diligent schoolboy. He was laboriously transcribing the *rules* to memorize them and perhaps to improve his handwriting, and spelling and capitalization rules in his time were different than modern styling.)

HANDWRITTEN NOTES

When you are writing to cheer someone or express gratitude, keep in mind that nothing can replace the intimacy of pen put to paper. In a computer-text-happy society where handwritten notes have been replaced by standardized fonts and a digital menu of emoticons, a well-crafted note written with a fine hand on good cotton or linen paper is a work of art. Take some time on your notes. When corresponding with an American diplomat in Europe, a frustrated George Washington wrote, "I will complain not only of your not writing, but of your writing so illegibly that I am half a day deciphering one page and then guess at much of it."[4]

In social correspondence, efficiency and politeness are inversely correlated, so no slap-dash envelopes, please. The addressee has an honorific, a first name, and a last name. Address your letter to "Mr. Pomeroy Fitzhugh," not to "Mr. Fitzhugh." Our first president would have been stumped by the title "Ms.," but he knew enough to caution us about respecting those honorifics. *In writing or Speaking, give to every Person his due Title According to his Degree & the custom of the Place,* he tells us in Rule 39.

George Washington's greetings displayed subtle gradations in tone. He addressed strangers as "Sir" and acquaintances as "Dear Sir." Very close friends received a "My dear Sir." He opened his letters to his mother with a formal "Honored Madam." Martha was favored with a "My dearest."[5]

A return address written by hand is more personal than a pre-printed label, and though metered mail is practical for wholesale business correspondence, a stamp gives an envelope the appeal that makes the recipient want to open it before all other mail.

TELEPHONE

Not long after Alexander Graham Bell spoke over the wire the famous words, "Come here, Mr. Watson, I want to see you," the telephone had become a popular mode of communication. However, telephone conversation (excluding Skype and similar video calls) lacks the visual clues involved in face-to-face contact and requires a high level of sensitivity and clarity. People who are polite in every other aspect of their lives are sometimes rude on the telephone.

Before you place a call, look at the clock. If it is before 9 a.m. or after 9 p.m., there is a good chance that someone is asleep. Any phone call in the middle of the night signals calamity. Who has not panicked with fears for a loved one's safety in the moments it takes to reach for the phone?

Unless the person you are calling answers the phone and immediately greets you by name (the wonders of caller identification), do not assume he recognizes your voice. Introduce yourself. If somebody else answers, greet him before asking for the person to whom you wish to speak: "Hi, Sam. This is Mary Jane. May I speak to Elisabeth?" If you are puzzled by an unexpected voice answering the phone, please do not blurt out, "Who is this?" After all, you initiated the call. Again, simply identify yourself and ask for the intended party. Hopefully, the other speaker will respond with his name.

When you place a call, be prepared for conversation. "Hold just a sec, I'm getting my mail and putting a leash on the dog" is not a way to greet the person who has stopped what she was doing to take your call.

Because telephone communication is purely verbal (no lip reading or hand gestures), it is important to speak clearly and in a well-modulated voice directly into the mouthpiece. George Washington knew this, though he never could have even imagined a telephone. Rule 73 states: *Think before you Speak pronounce not imperfectly nor bring out your Words too hastily but orderly & distinctly.*

If you have ever received a phone call with so much noise in the background that you were unable to hear your caller, you will understand the need to consider background interference before placing or receiving a call. What level of noise would be tolerable were your conversation partner sitting next to you? No matter how loud both parties scream, there is no way to compete with the pelting of a car wash, the bang of a jackhammer, or the blaring of a radio or television. And really, would you be flushing the toilet if the person were there with you?

When you leave a message, make it short and sweet. How many times have you replayed a slurred and rambling message and still failed to understand all of it? If you want a return call, the efficiencies of call records and contact lists notwithstanding, leave your number.

Many a relationship has been soured by the simple failure to return a phone call. We think we can guess the reason for the call, but we are often wrong. That yammering friend might be calling to tell you she is going into the hospital the following day. Someone else might be offering you last-minute tickets to a special event. Unless it is an unsolicited sales pitch or "robo" call, there are not many excuses for not returning a telephone call within twenty-four hours.

Smart Phones

Smart phones are invaluable to our busy lifestyles but provide myriad opportunities to irritate bystanders and message recipients. This includes the person you endangered in traffic because you were preoccupied with your phone and the innocent person who cannot quietly enjoy a magazine while riding next to you on the bus or waiting in the doctor's office.

If you must use a cell phone in public, keep your voice as low as possible. Do not broadcast endless intimate details of your life—"I told him if I caught him cheating one more time . . ."— or assess publicly the behavior of the party to whom you are speaking—"That is not normal; you need help." At all costs, avoid self-narration—"I am walking into the store"; "I am standing in line." Sorry, but no one will think you are cute, connected, or possessive of a great personality based on an overheard phone call. If he didn't anticipate the telephone, George Washington did anticipate the decline in peace and quiet, as Rule 24 shows us: *Do not laugh too loud or too much at any Publick Spectacle.* He might also have cautioned us against being a public spectacle ourselves.

Turn off your digital device when attending any public event. If you must leave it on, set the ringer to "vibrate" so that all chirps, chimes, beeps, pings, and buzzes are muted. Likewise, forget clandestinely texting or using your phone at all in a theater— your flashing and flickering screen will give you away every time.

Cyberspace

Cyberspace offers an efficient and far-reaching way to seamlessly link people across time and space, thereby shrinking the world, bridging gaps, and eroding natural barriers. By allowing constant dialogue and immediate feedback, this phenomenon has opened entirely new dimensions to relationship management. While perpetual availability to everybody you know can make communication more frequent, it can also make it less personal. It can intensify closeness or subvert it. Let cyberspace be a supplement, not a substitute for keeping in touch.

E-MAIL

E-mail is a great way to transmit a message, save time, and keep records. Electronic messages may be either as urgent as a phone call or as leisurely as a letter. It is informal: pens, letterhead, and the old polite greetings and turns of phrase are out the window. It is fast: no folding, licking, stamping, or walking to the mailbox. And it can be dangerous: pausing to rethink a message is not necessary, and outgoing e-mails disappear at the click of the mouse.

Before firing off an e-mail, hesitate and decide whether the correspondence is repetitive, confidential, or embarrassing should it fall into the wrong hands. "Forward" with caution and use "Reply All" sparingly.

When it comes to keeping in touch, fast and easy is not always better. A message blasted to multiple recipients is so easy that the recipient knows how little time and thought were required of the sender. When a "to a best friend" poem is sent to twenty-five people, it somehow loses its power. Before forwarding that hilarious cartoon, political diatribe, quote of the day, travelogue, or picture album, stop a moment and ask yourself, "Do I have any reason to think the recipient is interested?" "Am I boring or bragging?" "Is this too fast, too informal, and too ephemeral?"

THE DIGITAL AGE

In every time period and in every culture, human beings

have demonstrated a basic need to communicate and express themselves. Our interests beg to be recorded. Sixteen-year-old George Washington kept a travel diary of his expeditions across the Blue Ridge Mountains; and until his death, he continued to record innumerable details of farming and weather. Today, blogs, graphics, and videos have become the platform of choice. Locked diaries and day journals are rapidly becoming quaint relics of a more private era.

Legions of lonely folk find comfort in online communication. Conversely, myriad merrymakers find it an additional outlet for their social energies. However, as the delicate etiquette of online social norms has yet to be defined, social networking sites offer many opportunities for hurt feelings, damaged reputations, and unexpected or dangerous consequences. Do these sites foster human bonds, or do they foster anonymity? Are they facilitators or detractors of an active social life?

In every age, egoism has interfered with genuine social intercourse. Today, however, egoism seems to be running rampant. In pursuit of celebrity, ordinary people are donning shiny new online personas and reinventing themselves as television reality stars or Hollywood tabloid fodder. Even crazier, these fabulists actually come to believe in their false identities and think their moment of fame has arrived. If you find yourself tweeting the minutiae of your daily life ("I'm playing with my dog"; "I'm drinking a latte") or, even worse, documenting the blow-by-blow drama of your life, stop and reconsider this "me-me-me" clamor. As your mother said, "It's not all about you." Ask yourself how many times you have elicited the words of Rhett Butler: "Frankly, my dear, I don't give a damn"?

Get a grip. Preserve control of your online identity. Postings that seem private can scatter and slip unpredictably. Every word you write and every picture you post can be accessed by virtually everybody. Unless the postings are suitable viewing for family and for current or prospective employers and colleagues, keep them off your Facebook wall or in a very small Google+ circle. If you would not tell it to someone in person, why tell it to the world? Also, because photos can be unpredictably "tagged" with your name, periodically check your pages for incriminating evidence. The skeletons in your online closet may come back to haunt you at a later date.

The Internet is living proof of the adage "garbage in, garbage out." In blogs, posts, comment streams, and tweets, ill-informed speculation is often substituted for genuine expertise; and conspiracy theories and downright lies abound. Remember the game "Telephone"? One person whispers something to another person, who whispers to another, and so on. After going full circle, the original message is unrecognizable. In a similar fashion, after a blogger posts about what another blogger wrote about yet another blogger's response to a different blogger's commentary (and on as on, as the viral chain may lead), the end result is a crop of mixed truths, untruths, and falsehoods. We must learn how to sort and evaluate information, to make judgments about evidence and sources, and to separate the important from the trivial. Before accepting and passing on everything you read, slow down, be skeptical, and check it out. George saw this one coming a mile (and several centuries) away, and he warns us in Rule 79: *Be not apt to relate News if you know not the truth thereof.*

PRIVACY CONCERNS

Every new form of communication—from papyrus to printing press, from carrier pigeon to the United States Postal Service, from landline telephone to e-mail and cell phones—opens new opportunities for the invasion of privacy. Personal correspondence becoming public news has always been a concern. When in 1775 Benjamin Franklin introduced a decree to the Second Continental Congress for the creation of the United States Postal Service, he included a provision that forbade opening the mail of another person. Sometimes that rule has been followed; sometimes it hasn't.

Early on, resigning himself to the lack of postal privacy protection, Washington wrote, "As to my sentiments . . . I will disclose them without reserve (although by passing through the post offices, they should become known to all the world)."[6] Be certain of your sentiments when you publish them, because all the world *will* know them.

The next threat to privacy presented itself in the telephone. In the early days of the telephone, there was the snoopy operator (you have seen this in old movies), who listened long after connecting the two lines. And do you remember party lines? By surreptitiously picking up the phone, you could hear everything a neighbor said. Today, the speakerphone shares what you say with everyone in the room or car, and the answering machine replays your message to all with access to the recording.

As with the postal service and the telephone, cyberspace is adding new dimensions to our concern for privacy. Because we access cyberspace in the confines of our home or office, we often forget that as new technology adds to the ways we can connect, it also adds to the worries about our privacy. Beware of the confidentiality sieve! E-mails, social networking sites, and comment streams send conversations off in unintended directions. Today, everything from the hard drive of your computer to the log of your cell phone calls is being recorded.

Social networking sites especially have a tendency to breed a false sense of security. While offering an efficient and far-reaching way for people to meet, these sites have eroded natural barriers. Never forget, creeps are everywhere and can easily compile a dossier on you. The troll of childhood's "Three Billy

Goats Gruff" is a piker. It is the Internet trolls—the spammers, identity thieves, and phishers—that are the scariest of all.

FINAL THOUGHTS

Modern methods of communication have a grand tradition of distancing people from one another for the sake of efficiency. Talking on the phone replaced talking in person. Now texts, e-mails, and video conferences are taking the place of many phone conversations. Technology poses a threat we have not faced before. It allows so much speed, ease, and freedom that if we escape the "too little communication" group, we easily fall into "too much communication."

In truth, our "too much communication" is really only communication of a sort. We are sometimes so busy texting that we forget to talk, and often it seems that online friendship has ruined real friendship. Have you seen people sharing common space while tethered to their electronics? Rather than striking up a conversation with those nearby, they are talking to, tweeting, or texting people who are not there. If you are more available to your digital devices than you are to those around you, it is time to reprioritize: slow down, power down, and remove that ear piece. Those folks around you have every reason to feel annoyed—they are being ignored. Rarely is anything virtual so urgent that it should take precedence over flesh and blood. Relish the moment and "love the one you're with." If you absolutely must take a call or read a text, apologize to your companion and be brief. As George says in Rule 18: *Read no Letters, Books, or Papers in Company but when there is a necessity for the doing of it you must ask leave.*

No matter how "smart" your phone is or how tempting its thousands of new engaging applications, nothing surpasses that spark of fellowship and the indescribable feeling of togetherness that comes from face-to-face interaction. Intimacy cannot be replicated by a hashtag, photo, smiley face, or "U R Gr8" text. Real relationships need the context of the real world.

CHAPTER FOUR

Free Speech

Be not tedious in Discourse, make not many Digressings, nor
repeat often the Same manner of Discourse.

—Rule

God bless our Founding Fathers for championing the freedom of speech necessary for the free flow of ideas essential to a democracy! In 1783, George Washington preached to officers of the army, "If the freedom of speech is taken away then dumb and silent we may be led, like sheep to the slaughter."[1] Even in a time of war, our esteemed leader recognized that the beauty of a democracy is that everyone be given a chance to speak and be heard. But Washington also recognized that not all speech is equal or appropriate. Conversation is a cooperative activity:

a mutual exchange of ideas that enables us to work together to form a vibrant and caring community. We need to learn how to do it right.

TALKING TOO MUCH

George Washington is succinct and to the point in Rule 35: *Let your Discourse with Men of Business be Short and Comprehensive.* Washington's second inaugural address was only 135 words long and took less than two minutes to read. Do you chatter away for no rhyme or reason? Do you talk simply to hear yourself fill the void? The old adages "Don't talk unless you can improve the silence" and "If you keep your mouth shut, you won't put your foot in it" are good advice for the garrulous. Even if you have something substantive to say, you can easily drone on too long. Monologues are the opposite of the give-and-take of good conversation. Before lunging ahead, catch your breath, measure out your talk in manageable bits, and defer to another speaker.

Learning is best presented with quick wit, not long-winded pedantry. The raconteur can easily become a windbag, and jokes often fail when delivered to the wrong audience. Have you ever been forced to endure a twenty-minute anecdote that transforms a most extraordinary event into an incredibly boring one? What about suffering through a joke you have heard several times before? Do some people jabber so nimbly that you can't figure out what they are trying to say?

If you have carried on about your favorite subject for more than a couple of minutes, keep in mind Rule 80: *Be not Tedious in Discourse or in reading unless you find the Company pleased therewith.* Good conversation moves from one topic to another at a natural pace. A boring conversationalist stays on one subject for too long, a self-centered conversationalist interrupts discussion to change the subject, and a repetitive conversationalist bores by constantly saying the same things. Now and then, give yourself a "shush." If your company is pleased with your talk, they will show it. Do not wait for their glazed eyes to stop you.

Listening Up

Listening is usually more important than talking. If you pay attention to what someone says and do not interrupt, you might actually learn something. If nothing else, you will discover the particular needs, motivations, and hopes of those around you.

Washington was a masterful listener and understood the power of silence. He advised his adopted grandson, "where there is no occasion for expressing an opinion, it is best to be silent, for there is nothing more certain than that it is at all times more easy to make enemies than friends."[2]

Sometimes active listening requires withholding your responses. While talking along may mean you are enthusiastic about the subject, interjections can be and often are taken as a sign of impatience. Completing a colleague's sentence may show that you understand what he is saying, but it can also show that you do not. Even if you do understand what he is saying and know what he is going to say, interruption is jarring and rude. Wait your turn. Our first president chimes in on this topic with Rule 74: *When Another Speaks be attentive your Self and disturb not the Audience if any hesitate in his Words help him not nor Prompt him without desired, Interrupt him not, nor Answer him till his Speech be ended.*

Make eye contact so that the speaker knows you are interested and paying attention. Looking everywhere *except* at the speaker makes it clear that you are less than interested in whatever he has to say. Signal that you are following by responding with regular nods or short acknowledgments such as "right" or "yes."

Watching Your Language

In order to converse pleasantly, you must watch what you say. Take an inventory of your content and make an effort to clean it up. Do pleasant words come out of your mouth? The following words are magical, safe, and applicable to service people, coworkers, and friends:

"Please," when you ask for something.

"Thank you," when you receive it.

"Excuse me," when you have interrupted.

"I'm sorry," when you have offended.

Yes, you learned these in kindergarten, but think how many people do not use these simple words. However, remember that you are not the manners police. If others fail to say "please" or "thank you," it is not your place to ask, "What do you say?" or sarcastically respond, "You're welcome." Teach by example.

When you travel to a foreign country, learn how to say the above phrases in the language of the land. It is considerate and will endear you to the locals as well as make your trip more enjoyable. But when you return to the good old USA, leave those *bon mots* at the shore. Rule 72, *Speak not in an unknown Tongue in Company but in your own Language,* reminds us that dropping your handful of foreign words around those who do not speak that language will sound affected, and those who do speak the language are more likely to wince than be impressed.

If foul language tends to spew from your lips, remember Rule 49: *Use no Reproachfull Language against any one neither Curse nor Revile.* Unwilling to tolerate swearing, Washington warned that soldiers would receive twenty-five lashes for cursing and more severe punishment for a second offense.[3] Whether you are under stress or in an extremely relaxed mood, there is always a more effective and impressive way to make a point than by resorting to a litany of expletives.

In private letters and in public statements, Washington rejected intolerance, prejudice, and "every species of religious persecution." He hoped that "bigotry and superstition" would be overcome by "truth and reason"[4] in the United States. Although that hasn't happened yet, you can help the process along. Refer to people respectfully. An adult female is a "woman" or a "lady," not a "girl" or a "gal." An adult male is a "man," not a "boy" or a "bud." People of different ethnic origins can be particularly sensitive to terms that label or stereotype. Never display any shade of prejudice, and refrain from making patronizing or derogatory remarks about race or sex—or anything else, really.

Does your conversation default to warmed-over clichés? With repetition, expressions such as "busy as a bee," "open a can of worms," and "eat like a horse" have become hackneyed. If you mindlessly describe everything as "spectacular," "awesome," "fabulous," or "totally," your superlatives will lose their luster. What about catch phrases? How often do you pepper your sentences with "oh gosh," "dad gummit," "for Pete's sake," or "no problem"? Do your sentences drift to a "ta-da" conclusion?

"Ya know," "uhm," "er," "like," and "uh" are verbal tics. Break the habit of relying on these nervous fillers, and pause when you are searching for a word or trying to form your thoughts. Listeners often appreciate two or three seconds of silence, because it gives them time to digest what you've said. Never underestimate the power of dead air.

Modulate Your Tone

People may not remember what you say, but they will remember how you make them feel. An expression as simple as "How are you?" can range in inflection from breezy to earnest to gloomy and, as a result, can convey totally different meanings. Listen to your overall tone and volume. Do you whine? Do you shriek? Do you nag? Do you mutter? Are you too loud? Are you strident? Are you snippy? Do you bark like an army sergeant? Does your voice drip with exasperation? Does your grandiose manner of elocution stifle lively conversation? Spontaneity and surprise are basic to a free flow of words. Speak cheerfully and without airs, and everyone in earshot will thank you.

George Washington worked on keeping a positive outlook. In 1782, he commended a fellow officer for passing the time in a merry manner: "It is assuredly better to go laughing than crying thro' the rough journey of life."[5] To his ever crabby mother, he advised, "Happiness depends more upon the internal frame of a person's mind, than on the externals of the world."[6]

Some people just give up trying to be positive and instead take satisfaction in dragging others down with them. Have you found yourself retreating from that bitter guy who hates the crooked politicians, the greedy businessmen, and the stupid boss? Who finds the weather bad and the tax code unfair? These people are, in an expression coined by William Safire and spoken by Vice-President Spiro Agnew in 1970, "the nattering nabobs of negativism."

At the other end of the spectrum are the "butter-wouldn't-melt-in-her-mouth" sanctimonious poisoners. Their honeyed voices sound cloyingly cheerful and soft, but they take delight in pricking others' balloons, raining on others' parades, and spoiling others' fun. Smiling through their teeth, they put their inner bile on display as clearly as if they were complaining outright.

Sometimes you will be faced with the know-it-alls. These people have a sublime confidence about how to handle all situations. Their children are perfect, because they—of course—are the perfect parents. Concerning investments—they just "made a killing." Regarding home décor or fashion—just ask them; they are the experts. You will be tempted to pop their happiness balloons, especially if you know that their children

are less than stellar, their taste in clothes and furniture is out-
moded, and their finances are "iffy." But hold on to your needle.
A response of "oh, really" is safe and noncommittal.

Argument

George Washington might have been combative in war, but
in politics he demonstrated his ability to work through partial
arguments to the fundamental principles on which everyone
could agree. A witness at the First Continental Congress noted,
"He asks few questions, listens attentively, and answers in a
low tone with few words."[7] The forever modest Washington
portrayed his position as an "attentive observer and witness."[8]

In Rule 86, he writes, *In Disputes, be not So Desirous to
Overcome as not to give Liberty to each one to deliver his Opinion.*
The tradition of open polite discussion, successfully guiding
our country in earlier periods of history, has been replaced by a
coarser public discourse. The rancorous, overheated rhetoric of
radio and talk shows has become characterized by raised voices,
unpleasant arguments, vicious insults, and rude interruptions.

The new brawling style of argument in our public forums may
amuse or amaze, but it is no model for personal behavior. Leave
it to the media pundits to set up a verbal firing squad, and then
sit back to watch the carnage. Let them fan the flames and play
the "gotcha" games, and do not be that way yourself. Free speech
should not mean the freedom to harangue.

In one-on-one conversation, do not provoke unpleasantness or
contention; and if a debate or argument is thrust on you by another,
conduct yourself with restraint. Though it is tempting to pick up
the gauntlet when it is thrown down, do not be argumentative
simply for the sake of it. Washington wrote in 1781, "It is much
easier to avoid disagreement than to remove discontents."[9]

Do you relish being right about everything? Would you

wound a friend to gain a point? Does your favorite cause and your opinion about it so impassion you that you believe others must be converted to your way of thinking? If they are not convinced, do you see them as your enemy or feel that they have betrayed you personally? As Winston Churchill (half American and hence under the patrimony of the Father of Our Country) once said, "A fanatic is one who can't change his mind and won't change the subject."[10] The fanatic's path is a narrow and lonely one.

People who rave at others often think themselves "confident," "volatile," or "passionate," and they enjoy letting it fly. After working themselves up into a blood-boiling tizzy, they feel ever so much better. Because they feel fine, they assume those around them feel fine too, and that all is forgotten. However, despite the old children's taunt, a solid verbal browbeating often hurts just as much as "sticks and stones." If you subject people to vitriolic attacks, you are injuring them; and even if they love you, they are eventually going to back away.

Politics and religion can be scintillating subjects of substantive conversation, but in speaking of such matters, take extra care not to be bellicose or bruise feelings. Spats about religion and politics are pointless. In these areas, people have beliefs rather than opinions. People have a right—in this country a sacred right—to their own thoughts on both matters. Even with friends you know well, do not presume you will see eye-to-eye on all issues. Thorny topics from global warming to gay rights can turn formerly safe conversations into strident, divisive disagreements. Expressing your own views on the assumption that others share your values is snobbery and condescension. You may be proselytizing against the very thing they believe in or the very group to which they belong.

Thomas Jefferson said, "I never consider a difference of opinion in politics, in religion, in philosophy, as cause for withdrawing from a friend."[11] It is not necessary to be silent, but it *is* necessary to be careful, to know and acknowledge who you are talking to, and to be a friend. If both parties maintain a willingness to consider respectfully the views of the other, they can disagree without being disagreeable. You can even have a good time doing it. Remember the proverb "two reasonable minds can disagree." The secret is in the word "reasonable." Get your passions under control, and you can have many evenings of lively discussion.

MEA CULPA

Sometimes, despite your best efforts, you will mess up and have to apologize. Here again, it is important to do it right. A genuine apology states your transgression, accepts the blame for the folly, and presents a plan to make it right. As George Washington wrote to his niece, "It is better to offer no excuse than a bad one."[12] A phony apology is a self-pitying parade of guilt with no intention of reform. Unless you are sincerely contrite and intend to correct your error, the rambling and staged confessional, "I'm 'sorry' if I offended you," is only half-hearted.

FLATTERY AND CRITICISM

When we make direct comments to people about themselves, caution should be our watchword. Ultimately, one must be as careful with compliments as with criticism, as either can be taken in the wrong spirit. We tend to refrain from criticizing others, but extreme complimenting needs some tempering too. Flatterers have always been suspect. *Be no Flatterer, neither Play with any that delight not to be Play'd Withal,* cautions Rule 17. Good advice, but even Washington found it hard to follow and resorted to a little "apple polishing" in his youth. When he was twenty-four, he wrote a flattering letter to a British general even while denying doing so: "Don't think my Lord I am going to flatter. I have exalted sentiments of Your Lordship's character and revere your rank. . . . My nature is honest and free from guile."[13]

Sycophants want something from those they flatter, and they say what they must to get it. Do not flatter solely with the hope of placing yourself in someone's good graces. Such manipulative fawning is transparent, unattractive, and usually fools no one.

Even sincere compliments can be misunderstood. Do not, for example, compliment someone's reformation. Do not ask someone if she has lost weight or changed her hairstyle. She will think, "Was I fat?" or "Did my hair look bad before?" You may simply say, "You look great" or "I like your hair." Of course, someone whose transformation is dramatic (such as a dramatic loss of weight) may be eager to talk about it. Follow her lead.

If you are the recipient of a compliment, accept it. The best response is simple: "Thank you," "You have made my day," or "That makes me feel great." Saying "Do you really think so?" hints that you want a repetition of the praise. Self-deprecation, such as "Oh, I think I look heavy in this," rejects the token of goodwill. You may respond with a compliment: "Thank you. So do you!" However, be honest. Do not simply invent something because you feel obligated.

Most of us understand that outright criticism is bad form and tends to hurt. Is there really such a thing as "constructive criticism"? If you have a tendency to needle others with suggestions for improvement, ask yourself, "Am I condescending? Is this kind? Is this helpful?"

Hopefully, we all already follow Rule 76, *While you are talking, Point not with your Finger at him*, and would not admonish someone by wagging a finger in his face. When you must offer a well-intentioned correction, avoid starting the sentence with

"You always." Say instead, "Have you considered . . . ?" This can effectively redirect your prickly speech toward a more positive, less accusatory expression of the message.

George Washington reminds us to keep the sting out of our conversation in Rule 47: *Mock not nor Jest at any thing of Importance break no Jest that are Sharp Biting and if you Deliver any thing witty and Pleasent abstain from Laughing there at yourself.* Sarcasm may feel clever at the moment you use it, but it is never endearing and rarely even effective. Snark, like sarcasm, celebrates the power to ridicule. This includes teasing. Step lightly here. Barbs that might be amusing during a casual get-together of good friends can wound deeply when delivered at a sensitive time or in a less private setting.

FINAL THOUGHTS

Not so long ago, fireside chats and congenial Sunday afternoons spent in conversation were a way of life. American humorist Mark Twain quipped, "It does not matter whether one talks wisdom or nonsense, the case is the same, the bulk of the enjoyment lies in the wagging of the gladsome jaw and the flapping of the sympathetic ear."[14]

Whatever happened to that easy stream of conversation? Today, with multi-directional pulls for our attention, we fear that if we concentrate on one thing—the subject at hand—we will miss what else is going on. Fast and furious, we interrupt, we blather, and we fail to listen.

Good conversation should be second nature to Americans. The fundamental secret of talking with others is simply to view each other, treat each other, and speak to each other as we are— equals who deserve genuine respect.

CHAPTER FIVE

The Good Sport

When you deliver a matter do it without passion & with discretion,
however mean the person be you do it too.

—Rule 83

The first organized athletic competition, the Olympics, was established in Greece almost 3,000 years ago. One of the most commonly held theories is that King Iphitos of Elis founded the games to honor the gods, as well as to promote peace among warring countries. All fighting had to cease during the competition so that the gods would not be offended. An olive branch, a symbol of peace, was bestowed on the winner of each event.

Unfortunately, in today's professional sports and even in youth organizations, the primordial urge to win, vanquish our opponents, and let everybody know about it takes control. In the heat of the game, we regularly witness anything but "champion" behavior in spectators as well as in players.

George Washington, a man accustomed to being first—"First in war, first in peace and first in the hearts of his countrymen"[1]— can teach us a lot about sportsmanship. Wherever and however we choose to play—on the field, in the stands, at the gym, in front of the television, or with a video game at home—we have a chance to practice good sportsmanship. For a sporting event to become a truly exhilarating, shared experience, we must keep a level playing field by practicing control, having heart, and being fair.

On the Field

A true sportsman is fiercely competitive yet behaves with dispassionate calm. He appears to be having fun even when performing badly. In the moment, this is much, much easier said than done. It requires real self-mastery to enter the game with your psyche in good order and keep your emotions in check during and after the game. The ultimate strategist, Washington learned to mask his interior emotions. When a woman remarked that she could see the joy in his face at his impending retirement from the presidency, he barked, "You are wrong! My countenance never yet betrayed my feelings."[2]

PLAYING FAIR

Being a good sport is all about fair play. A true sportsman never cheats. But is there anyone alive who has *never* cheated? Cheating does not have to be active. Have you ever, for example, let stand a call that you knew was wrong because it was in your favor? For most of us, it is too late to claim perfection. If asked, "What, never?," an honest reply for the majority would be, "Well, hardly ever!"

Even George Washington occasionally fudged victory when, in fact, there was none. After the Battle of Brandywine in 1777, Washington spread the story that the British troops had suffered more casualties than the Americans. In truth, the Americans had lost twice as many soldiers, but Washington did not think the colonists could hear this and still support the revolution.

There may be joy in winning dishonestly, but it is not the joy of sport. The joy of sport involves embracing the risk of loss. Cheaters, by contrast, do not take the risk. They are fixers. They rig the game, doing whatever it takes to guarantee themselves a win.

The honest sportsman plays with openness and candor. He believes that without fair play there is no winner. He plays by the rules no matter who is looking. The cheater manipulates appearances and does anything he can get away with in order to win. If you are honorable, cheating will only make you feel miserable. If you are a cheater, you may scorn the rule-bound; but in taking an unfair advantage, you will always be the loser. The good news is that it is never too late to play fair.

PLAYING YOUR POSITION

Undertake not to Teach your equal in the art himself Professes; it Savours of arrogancy, advises Rule 41. Good, as well as not so good, players can slip unconsciously into teaching mode. Even if you are the most skilled player on the team, you are not the coach. And who wants an impromptu lesson from an average teammate? Never give another player unsolicited advice before, during, or after a game. As Rule 68 reminds: *Give not Advice without being Ask'd & when desired do it briefly.*

"Teaching" during or after play sometimes takes on an ugly edge. There is nothing forgivable about berating another player for a mistake, especially in front of others. Recriminations simply have no place in sport. If critiquing others is a habit for you, shut it down. It is excruciatingly painful and dreary for everyone when any player tells another how he *should* have done things.

Losing and Winning Gracefully

Sometimes you win; sometimes you lose. Whether you win or lose, respect everyone. When the game is finished, shake hands and say, "Nice game." Never refuse to shake hands when you lose, even if you believe you were wronged in some way.

If you lose, accept your defeat with grace. Congratulate your opponent for his play. Do not say, "I played badly today." Such a statement shows a refusal to accept defeat and translates as "I'm a better player and would have beaten you if I hadn't had an off day." It denigrates your opponent's success by attributing it to your own momentary lapse.

In Rule 22, Washington advises, *Shew not yourself glad at the Misfortune of another though he were your enemy.* If you win, accept victory with modesty. Do not "rub it in" by being a show-off or indulging in arrogance and boasting. Let your opponent congratulate you—do not congratulate yourself. Refrain from celebratory dancing. When asked why he did not celebrate in the end zone after each of his many touchdowns, NFL great Barry Sanders responded that he did not want to look as if he had never been in the end zone and would never be there again.

In the Stands

Before baseball existed in its modern form, Americans played cricket. By the time of the American Revolution, cricket was so popular that General Washington, hoping to improve morale after the devastating winter at Valley Forge, allowed his troops to play. A first lieutenant wrote in his diary, "This day his Excellency (Washington) did us the honor to play wicket with us."[3] If George Washington were president today, would he be able to throw the ball in a ceremonial pitch at Opening Day, the All Star Game, or the World Series? Though the power of George Washington's arm was legendary, his throwing a silver coin a mile across the Potomac is a myth. It is more likely that he hurled or skipped rocks an impressive 250 feet across the Rappahannock River at his childhood home Ferry Farm.

Football, baseball, basketball, and soccer have replaced cricket in popularity today, and all are great reasons for a good "hip hip hooray!" If it involves a ball, we become passionate. Loyal fans hash out strategies and share stories of games past. Enthusiasts festoon themselves with team insignia, clothe themselves in team colors, and even paint their faces to match.

Passion notwithstanding, remember you are a representative of the team, and your deportment reflects positively or negatively on it. Sing that fight song. Make the stadium roar. Hoot and holler; raise a ruckus. It is fun to be a passionate fan. However, remember that working yourself up to an unmediated level of fury does nothing to rally your team and is certainly nothing of which to be proud. Ball games create an intimate environment, and any misbehavior intensifies in the crowded setting of an arena or stadium. You can cheer for your team without taunting or demeaning the opposing side. Be passionate and have fun, but be respectful.

Irrespective of allegiances, a true sports aficionado admires any extraordinary athletic feat. Respect all players and coaches; they have practiced and worked hard. Whether your team wins or loses, applaud their efforts. Practice Rule 44: *When a man does all he can though it Succeeds not well blame not him that did it.* Let the coaches coach, the officials officiate, and the players play. Do not trash the competition, hiss, or boo. There is always another season and another chance.

AT THE GYM

The gym was originally the domain of jocks, weightlifters, and basketball and football players. Today, due to a heightened national awareness of fitness, the gym is part of the daily routine for millions of Americans. Whether working with a personal trainer or meeting people in fitness classes or in the weight-room, we build relationships as well as muscles when we work out.

Keeping fit was also important to our first president. Washington's physical prowess was renowned. A fellow officer observed that the commander-in-chief was thought to be the strongest man in the army. After undergoing surgery to remove a tumor in his thigh, Washington was unable to exercise and felt the lack keenly. He wrote in an overdramatic strain, "The want of regular exercise with the cares of office will, I have no doubt, hasten my departure for that country from whence no traveler returns."[4]

THE EXERCISE ROOM

Using exercise equipment is an exercise in sharing. The machine you are on may be your favorite, but it is not yours to monopolize. If others are waiting for a turn, relinquish it after a reasonable time. Do not place towels or other belongings on equipment to "reserve" it or, more accurately, "hog" it for later use while you take a class or lift weights. Remember to put your weights back on the rack. Because you are there to exercise, count the clean-up as part of the routine. For safety and cleanliness, wipe off the equipment after use.

EXERCISE CLASS

Traditional classroom rules apply to exercise class. If you are late to class, enter with as little disruption as possible. This includes taking off your outerwear and putting on your sneakers before entering. Find a place that will not crowd other participants or block their view of the mirror.

Exercise class has a social aspect, but do not chat too much while others are trying to concentrate. Practice good breathing, but avoid making additional sounds that might disrupt others. Follow the instructor's directions. If you cannot do so, wait out that particular segment. Do not do your own thing, because it will irritate the instructor and confuse other members of the class.

LOCKER ROOM

George Washington may not have spent much time in a locker room, but he was very accustomed to sharing cramped quarters with other people. Modesty, which was such a mark of Washington's character, should serve as an example to us when showering or dressing at the gym. Be mindful that you are sharing intimate space with other people and heed Rule 7: *Put not off your cloths in the presence of others.* In other words, respect other people's privacy and your own by not parading around naked. Or as George stated more directly in Rule 3, *Shew Nothing to your Freind(sic) that might affright him.*

FINAL THOUGHTS

Whether you are good at sports or not, be a good sport in life. In the face of personal adversity, the good sport knows how to courageously set his course and sail full speed ahead. Though your colleagues may be anxiously jostling for position in the workplace, you should promote teamwork, which values cooperation and strengthens connections.

Some people, like George, are blessed with natural athletic prowess. For the rest of us, it takes practice. So let us pat ourselves on the back once in a while and say, "nice game." At the finish, if we have learned to play hard, play fair, play courteously, and accept our victories and losses with grace, we can hold our heads high and feel like the champions we have become.

CHAPTER SIX

Our Best Foot Forward

In your Apparel be Modest and endeavour to accommodate Nature, rather than to procure Admiration; keep to the Fashion of your equals, Such as are Civil and orderly with respect to Times and Places.

—Rule 52

In less democratic societies, clothes clearly indicate occupation, rank, and gender. In America, individualism as expressed in one's choice of attire is given full sway. Preps and punks, dandies and dudes all have a place. It would be boring if we all relied on status-indicating uniforms or were denied flamboyance. Remember, however, that discretion is the better part of glamour; and if what you are wearing will likely embarrass your friends, your co-workers, or your family, you might be advised to think twice.

No matter how fashionable your outfit, there is no style in wrinkles, stains, odors, safety pins, torn armholes, or sagging hems. With the advent of home washing machines and dry cleaners on every corner, it should go without saying that, like your person, all your clothes should be clean and kempt. To repeat George Washington's Rule 51:*Wear not your Cloths, foul, unript or Dusty but See they be Brush'd once every day at least and take heed that you approach not to any Uncleaness.* Remember how much harder it must have been for people in his day to live by this rule!

THE MESSAGE OF MEN'S DRESS

Washington was well aware of the symbolism of personal attire and knew how to dress for the occasion, following Rule 52: *Keep to the Fashion of your equals Such as are Civil and orderly with respect to Times and Places.* When the Second Continental Congress assembled, he demonstrated Virginia's willingness to aid Massachusetts in fighting the British by being the only delegate in military uniform. For his first inauguration, President Washington wore an American-made brown broadcloth suit with eagle-adorned buttons. This plain attire, unlike that of a monarch in royal robes, signified that Washington was elected of, by, and for the people.

Whether riding to the hounds, dancing with the ladies, leading his troops to battle, or conducting the business of government, George Washington had a simple, two-fold requirement for his clothes—elegance and freedom of movement. He directed his tailor "to make it in the best taste to sit easy and loose, as clothes that are tight always look awkward and are uneasy to the wearer."[1]

In modern America, weddings, funerals, job interviews, and even some parties often demand that even the most casual of men wear a suit or sports coat. Nonetheless, even a fabulous jacket does not look so fabulous if it does not fit. When you try on a coat, check that the shoulder pads end with your shoulders and that the sleeves fall around where your thumb meets your wrist. When your arms are at your side, your knuckles should be even with the bottom of your jacket. The top button of the two-button suit or the middle button of the three-button suit should align with your bellybutton. And finally—the easy tip—never button that bottom button.

The shirt is the foundation of a well-dressed man, and a coat and tie does not mask a frayed collar or a coffee stain. A clean shirt of good fabric is always fashionable, but proper fit remains important. Is your shirt stretched out at the buttons? Is your long sleeve cuff riding above your wrist?

Some men willingly embrace ties, while others grudgingly accept that they must occasionally wear one. Though the necktie seems to have no practical purpose, its presence, for better or for worse, connotes class, wealth, power, eccentricity, or even humor. However, to achieve the desired effect, the tie must be in balance with the rest of one's attire. The width of the tie is determined by its proportion to the jacket lapel and shirt collar. As clothing designers modify the width of coat lapels, the width of the tie expands or shrinks accordingly. Similarly, the size of the tie knot reflects the changing collar widths. Too small a knot is lost in a wide collar, while too large a knot unnaturally spreads a small collar. One aspect of tie fashion remains constant—the length of the tie should be just long enough to reach the top of the belt buckle.

The tie may have only ceremonial status, but other items of men's attire have more functional purposes. Belts hold up pants; suspenders hold up pants. Since they perform the same function, they should not be worn together.

The wigs of colonial days and the fedora and bowler hats of the last century have been replaced by casual caps. Casual is fine, but remember that the old rules for headgear still apply. Take off that baseball cap when you are inside! You cannot just turn the visor backwards. Exceptions may be made for lobbies, corridors, sporting events, and sports bars. Otherwise, doff!

If you want an instant clue as to whether a person is well-dressed, look down. The twelve inches from the floor to mid-calf are the most indicative of a person's real situation. Hence, the term "well-heeled" marks the prosperous, and "down at the heel" indicates the impoverished—and these terms have literal roots. Scruffy shoes and sagging socks make a poor platform. Keep your shoes polished and maintain evenly worn heels.

George Washington lived in an age when male dress was more flamboyant, but can you imagine the president of the United States adorned with diamond earrings and gold chains? The dignified man limits his accessories to a fine watch and a signet, wedding, or college ring. Unless you aspire to hip-hop status, skip the bling. Real or not, jewelry on a man tends to look fake.

THE ELOQUENCE OF WOMEN'S DRESS

A woman does not need a bulging closet to dress well. Clothes derive their beauty from nice fabric, good lines, and a flattering fit. To develop your individual style, you have to know what makes you feel good and happy and incorporate these elements into your wardrobe. Personal flair lies in the twist of the scarf, the cut of the garment, and the imaginative mix of colors and textures.

Avoid blindly following someone else's fashion advice. Peer pressure and a constant bombardment from the media to have what other people have and to want what other people want have encouraged many of us to conform slavishly to ideals we cannot approach without damaging our pocketbooks or our bodies. People with true style know what works for them and what does not. Rule 52 again offers timeless advice: *In your Apparel be Modest and endeavor to accomodate Nature rather than to procure Admiration.*

A piece of jewelry brings a little sparkle to any outfit, but do not get carried away and think you have to empty your jewelry box every time you get dressed. As with all dress, the key is to achieve balance and proportion. If your necklace is big, your earrings should be small. If your earrings are big, your necklace should be small or nonexistent.

"Less is more" truly applies to perfume—a dab of perfume is usually enough. Be sensitive to other people's perfume allergies, and do not overload on scent when you are going to be in close quarters (such as a long car ride) or sitting alongside others for an extended period (as at the theater).

Overly revealing attire—body-hugging T-shirts, low-cut halter tops, and thigh-high skirts—has become more common in recent years, but so much exposure remains controversial. What constitutes enough clothing depends on where you are, what you are doing, how old you are, and what kind of shape you are in. If you turn up at no-nonsense functions wearing anything too short, too low-cut, or too tight, you will get attention, but not the right kind. At a ladies' luncheon, you can expect glares; at your child's school, you will be the subject of teachers' gossip; and in a business meeting, you will be treated as an annoying distraction.

One of the Founding Mothers, the straitlaced Abigail Adams, was horrified by the daringly low-cut dresses worn by the women at parties in Philadelphia. "The style of dress . . . is really an outrage upon all decency," wrote Abigail. "Most (ladies) wear their clothes scant upon the body and a little too full upon the bosom for my fancy."[2]

Restraint—the subtle art of knowing when enough is enough—should guide your decision on how much skin to bare. It is probably too much to highlight your breasts and your shapely legs at the same time. Save that mini skirt for another day.

George Washington warns us about the dangers of playing clotheshorse in Rule 54: *Play not the Peacock, looking everywhere about you, to See if you be well Deck't, if your shoes fit well if your Stockings sit neatly, and Cloths handsomely.* You may look marvelous, but if you want to put your best foot forward, respect the occasion and get over yourself. No matter how good you look, preoccupation with your appearance is a surefire style-spoiler. Checking your beauty in mirrors, adjusting your blouse, flipping your hair, pausing in doorways, asking others how you look, or cataloguing the details of your clothes for others all make you look like a desperate diva-wanna-be. If you are busy admiring yourself, no one else will bother.

BODY LANGUAGE

Run not in the Streets, neither go too slowly nor with Mouth open go not Shaking yr Arms kick not the earth with yr feet, go not upon Toes, nor in a Dancing fashion.

—Rule 53

It is picture time and the world is watching. Is our portrait complete? Not quite yet. We hear it so often: "You never have a second chance to make a first impression." The way we carry ourselves, our mannerisms, the expression on our face, and the way we walk, stand, or sit—all can complete our style or ruin it. We may be beautifully turned-out, but if we are slumping, fidgeting, sniffling, or glowering, our projection of "style" loses all meaning.

POSTURE

George Washington regarded a person's demeanor as the outward sign of inner order. "Nothing contributes so much to the appearance of a soldier, or so plainly indicates discipline, as an erect carriage, firm step, and steady countenance," he advised.[3]

Stand up straight, and whether you are too tall, too short, too stout, or too slim will become secondary. Good posture is an alignment of your ears, shoulders, and hips. Pretend that a helium balloon is attached to the top of your head and is pulling you upwards. In private, press your sternum, and you will feel your chest, shoulders, and head falling into place. Best of all, hit the gym, build some core strength, and your muscles will hold you erect. Head up, shoulders down.

A good walk reflects purpose, energy, and vigor. Walk with a light step and erect body. Dragging or shuffling your feet conveys laziness. An arrogant swagger demonstrates a cocky, overbearing confidence. The strutting popinjay is distinguished only by his vanity.

When you Sit down, Keep your Feet firm and Even, without putting one on the other or Crossing them, reads Rule 10. Even in these relaxed times, it is best to keep your knees together and at least one foot on the floor. Leg sprawl is indolent and vulgar. If you tend to forget, lock your ankles.

Facial Expression

A comrade-in-arms wrote of George Washington, "In conversation he looks you full in the face, is deliberate, deferential and engaging. His demeanor at all times composed and dignified."[4] Washington clearly kept in mind the simple formula of Rule 19: *Let your countenance be pleasant but in Serious Matters Somewhat grave.*

Like George, let your facial expression reflect the tone of the situation. If the subject is serious, a nervous laugh or tight-lipped smile is a disconcerting contrast. Likewise, if the mood is casual and relaxed, a rigid and tense expression can cause a negative change in the atmosphere. A frozen facial expression, whether of happiness or misery, is always unsettling. The sad sack's sullen and gloomy expression conveys anger and a sour disposition and brings everyone down. Equally unsettling is the ecstatic rapture and beatific smile of someone either conversing with the angels or overdosed on antidepressants. And whatever you are feeling, do not smirk! A smirk may be more insulting than an outright statement that you think someone is a fool. In Rule 12, George Washington warns, *Roll not the Eyes, lift not one eyebrow higher than the other, wry not the mouth.* You can fill in the rest.

If you have a tendency to leave your jaw hanging open, think of the dignified portraits of George Washington with his mouth firmly closed. Holding the mouth ajar makes a person look dopey, spacey, and ready to catch the next fly to come buzzing too close. If these reasons are not enough, remember that a mouth ajar and bad breath go hand in hand.

Final Thoughts

George Washington's authority began with his imposing physical presence. Standing six feet, two inches tall, buffed and polished, our hero looked resplendent in uniform. With an elegant sword strapped to his side and silver spurs attached to his boots, he cut a formidable figure. Founding Father Benjamin Rush declared him to be so distinguished that there was "not a king in Europe that would not look like a *valet de chambre* by his side."[5]

We have jettisoned many a clothing rule to free ourselves for self-expression in dress. However, Casual Friday notwithstanding, there will always be a difference between work clothes, play clothes, and dress-up clothes. The rules about when, where, and how to wear each may be subtle, but they are also well understood on almost a subconscious level. Make the effort. Dress the part. Present the best version of yourself in a way that shows respect for the people around you. The true you, dressed and groomed appropriately, is worth knowing. Your clothes, facial expression, and posture will go a long way toward opening doors and keeping them open.

CHAPTER SEVEN

At The Table

Be not Angry at Table whatever happens & if you have reason to be so, Shew it not but (put) on a Chearfull Countenance especially if there be Strangers for Good Humour makes one Dish of Meat a feast.

—Rule 105

America has always been the land of plenty, but our hasty, fast-food lifestyle leaves us hungry for something more than calories. In a country where tasty meals in a box abound, it is sometimes difficult to find time to gather around a nicely set table, use a proper knife and fork, and enjoy the conviviality of a sociable repast. Yet good talk over good food can be a wonderful, civilizing center of the day. One visitor to Mount Vernon observed, "George Washington would sit an hour after dinner in a familiar conversation and convivial hilarity."[1] Yes, he was a busy man, but he knew how to savor the pleasures of food and companionship.

Not all dinners need be elaborate occasions. The meal does not have to be fancy, or even homemade. The simplest fare, when served and eaten in a pleasant, well-mannered fashion, can turn into a memorable, shared experience. Washington relished the company of a "few social friends at a cheerful board."[2] Inviting a friend to visit, he wrote, "My manner of living is plain. I do not mean to be put out of it. A glass of wine and a bit of mutton are always ready, and such as will be content to partake of them are welcome."[3]

To restore moments of togetherness, try bringing communal meals back into your life. In an increasingly fragmented society, a dinner shared presents a splendid opportunity for sustenance as well as conversation. Bad manners, by contrast, will sour any meal, from the simplest fare to the most lavish feast.

What place do rules of good table manners have in the modern world? Self-conscious, nose-in-the-air, crooked-pinky table manners—"fancy" table manners, if you will—seem as outdated as finger bowls and as irrelevant as escargot forks. Simple common sense, though, underlies table manners. The rules of communal dining may seem arbitrary, but they are not merely ceremonial. Ask George Washington. Seventeen of the *Rules of Civility* that he painstakingly memorized dictate ways to keep the experience of eating focused on the pleasure of the food and the company, not on the distractions and distresses introduced by thoughtless diners. To discuss all seventeen rules one at a time would be too much. Fortunately, they are all based on four indispensable and practical principles: *cooperation, cleanliness, composure,* and *conversation.* If we understand and live by these principles, good table manners will come naturally.

Cooperation

Good table manners are not about hunger or efficiency; they assume you have enough time to eat and enough food so you do not have to compete for it. Fortunately, abundant food supplies and regular meals are a given for many Americans. By making cooperation and consideration the hallmark of our time at table, we can savor every morsel and moment.

Unless the food is plated by a third party, the first challenge in dining with good manners is getting the food from the serving dish to one's plate. The buffet offers a sumptuous array of food choices, and the family table is laden with platters and bowls of food. Both styles of dining present many chances to misstep.

The Buffet Line

Many people compare diners at the buffet line to pigs at the trough. The bad reputation of the buffet crowd stems from that fellow who muscles his way to the front and delays the line as he tries to make a decision. He nibbles a sample here and there, cuts in half the pre-proportioned items, fingers the bread, and leaves a trail of spilled food down the serving table. With plate heaped high, happy and oblivious, he heads to his table.

In a buffet setting, it is best to use the serving utensils provided. When serving yourself finger food, touch only the piece you intend to take. Pawing through the common bowl or basket is uncouth. Accept the portion offered. For example, if pieces of cake are put out, take one; do not cut it in half and put the other half back.

Several trips to the buffet line work better than trying to get "all you can eat" in one major forage. In a restaurant or club, take a clean plate for each visit to the buffet and let the busboy retrieve your dirtied one. Get your salad, return for your entree, and, last but not least, enjoy the desserts.

FAMILY STYLE

"Pass the peas, please" sounds like an easy request, but in family-style dining, your response to this request is riddled with chances to mess it up.

At the beginning of the meal, all food is passed counterclockwise to the right. The logic to this is that if the food is on your left side, it is easier to reach with your right hand. (Sorry, lefties.) The dance begins when you want a second helping. If food is out of reach, ask the person nearest it to pass it to you. At this point, the direction of passing is of no concern. If food is on its way to someone else, do not grab some as it goes by. Likewise, when passing salt and pepper (they are always passed together, even if only one has been requested), the original requester should be able to use the shakers first.

Keep greed in check. George Washington's Rule 91 reminds us, *Feed not with Greediness*. Take your portion from the edge of the serving dish closest to you, and do not dig around for the best piece or skim off more than your share of garnishes, crusty toppings, or other favorite bits. Offer others seconds before serving more for yourself, especially if it is the last portion. Never eat anything directly from the serving dish!

Cleanliness

It's unbecoming to Stoop much to one's meat. Keep your Fingers clean & when foul wipe them on a Corner of your Table Napkin.
—Rule 96

Getting food from the plate to the mouth can be messy. One goal of good table manners is to avoid dirtying the table or oneself. It also makes good sense when around food to keep our germs to ourselves. Wash your hands and clean your nails before meals.

Once you are seated with food on your plate, the trick is to get the food to your mouth without splattering, spilling, and generally making a mess of the table, your neighbors, or yourself. Bending close to the rim of your plate or raising your plate to your lips is not the solution. Sit up straight and keep those proverbial "elbows off the table." Bring your food to your mouth, not your mouth to the food. If you are unable to lift the food to your mouth neatly, take less on your fork.

Lest we think behavior at the table has only recently gone to the dogs, look to George Washington's Rule 90: *Being Set at meat Scratch not neither Spit Cough or blow your Nose except there's a necessity for it.* Do keep your nose, hands, and mouth off of other people's food. Unless it is offered to you, never take a bite of someone else's food or sip someone else's beverage. Likewise, refrain from double dipping. Once you have bitten a chip or vegetable, do not re-dip.

If you love that bread basket, remember the expression "to break bread," or better yet, apply Rule 92: *Take no Salt or cut Bread with your Knife Greasy.* Rather than bite from a whole roll or slice, use your fingers to break off a bite-sized piece. If butter is served from a shared dish, take a pat and put it on your plate or bread plate. Butter the bread, not all at one time, but as you eat it.

The choice of whether to use fingers or a knife and fork is sometimes a question of sauce and setting. For example, when bacon or asparagus is crisp and the setting informal, it is okay to pick them up to eat. On the other hand, though pizza and sandwiches are considered finger foods, they are often so large that they need to be cut to a manageable size to fit in the mouth. When the choice is not clear, let the formality of the setting lead the choice. No matter how informal the occasion, neatness counts. Dripping, slobbering, splattering, and shoving too-large quantities of food into the mouth are never pleasant to watch, hear, or clean up after.

COMPOSURE

Sharing is the hallmark of a good meal, but nasty sounds and ugly sights are better kept to yourself. Even small, unconscious habits can become really offensive when people are trying to eat. Though crunching, slurping, smacking, snuffling, snorting, and burping may express satisfaction and do no actual harm, your fellow diners do not want to hear these sounds. Nor do they want to decipher what you are saying while your mouth is full. Swallow first and converse only with an empty mouth. Remember, as George writes in Rule 98, *Drink not nor talk with your mouth full.*

Rule 97 addresses gluttony: *Put not another bit into your Mouth til the former be Swallowed let not your Morsels be too big for the Gowls.* Unless you are a chipmunk hoarding nuts for the winter, put in your mouth only the portion that you are able to chew gracefully. And, unless you are a cow, eat with your mouth closed.

Nervous sound effects—tapping your feet on the floor, drumming fingers on the table, pinging the rim of your glass, and humming under your breath—disturb a peaceful meal. A senator from rural Pennsylvania complained of a fidgeting

Washington, "At every interval of eating, he played on the table with a fork or knife, like a drumstick."[4] Like George, you might be bored or restless, but no one wants to watch you mindlessly reduce your paper napkin to shreds, herd little piles of bread crumbs around the tablecloth, or arrange cherry stems or olive pits into designs on your plate. If you are so nervous that your hands must constantly be doing something, wring them unseen in your lap.

If you must use a toothpick, excuse yourself from the table and use it in private. Watching someone excavate his teeth is not a pretty sight. Likewise, sometimes you will have no choice but to sneeze into your napkin, but never use your napkin as a handkerchief. Rule 5 suggests, *If you must Cough, Sneeze, Sigh, or Yawn, do it not Loud but Privately.*

"Excuse me, I am going to powder my nose," women used to say when leaving for the restroom. This expression is heard less often these days, as more people perform grooming rituals at the table. Although it might be acceptable to quickly freshen one's lipstick during a meal, fussing with hair and fixing that damaged nail are still best practiced away from the table.

Rule 95 directs, *Spit forth* (no) *stones of any fruit Pye upon a Dish not Cast anything under the table.* Dramatic demonstrations should be saved for genuine emergencies such as choking or having an allergic reaction. Otherwise, if you cannot swallow something in your mouth, make as little of the event as possible by simply returning the item to the plate in the same way it left it. For example, something small like an olive pit or fish bone can be delicately removed with fingertips or dropped onto an open palm, but a piece of bone or gristle is better retrieved with a fork. (If the offending object is unsightly, you may discreetly use a napkin to get it out of your mouth and hide it for the rest of the meal.)

CONVERSATION

If others talk at Table be attentive but talk not with Meat in your Mouth.

—Rule 107

The most pleasant conversation comes naturally, or appears to, and includes everyone at the table. If you are quiet, participate at least a little; if you are talkative, give others a chance to speak. Sullen silences and moralistic monologues are both dreary. Needless to say, aggressive rants or red-faced, angry arguments about religion and politics are hardly helpful.

Once the flow of conversation gets going, try not to break the mood. The host may lead a blessing before a meal, but if he or she does not, do not take the initiative yourself. God will hear your silent prayer. Is your piety a sufficient reason to make others feel remiss for not having given their thanks out loud or uncomfortable if they do not share your beliefs?

Ironically, one of the worst mood-breakers is pointing out other people's lapses in manners. Do not be a prig. You may know the rules, but turn a blind (or at least a forgiving) eye to other people's manners during the meal itself. If you cannot avoid noticing, at least refrain from inserting lectures or reminders into the conversation. Even with children, a constant chorus of "stop that" and "don't do that" will often achieve less than a quiet reminder.

A topic lately risen to unpleasant prominence at meals is diet. We all know that giving detailed descriptions of medical procedures at the table is not appetizing, but discussion of endless dietary matters—organic or non-organic, triglycerides, the impact of sugar, or the newest weight-loss rage—also distracts from the joy of food. Since many people have food allergies, requiring a meal with no gluten, no dairy, or no nuts, a wise host will ask dinner party guests about any special dietary restrictions in advance. However, unless you are being forced to eat something that is going to make you turn red, stop breathing, or be sent to the hospital, do not complain about items on the menu or announce your finicky tastes. If you are a picky eater and have been served something that makes you a bit queasy, remember the childhood trick of cutting the food into little pieces and moving it around on your plate.

In colonial days, the average American drank a pint of beer or several glasses of wine with meals. Though he certainly consumed his share, Washington once complained that Williamsburg life was a continual round of dinners and that "it is not possible for a man to retire sober." After retiring to Mount Vernon, he told one visitor that Virginians were "less given to intoxication . . . it is no longer fashionable for a man to force his guests to drink and make it an honor to send them home drunk."[5]

It remains unfashionable to pressure anyone to eat or drink. Avoid expressions such as "You have to try this," or "Trust me, you'll like it." You do not know why they are not having something, and it is rude to make them explain.

THE PERFECT ENDING

Most people know that they should wait to eat until the hostess sits and takes the first bite. Sometimes the hostess will suggest that you eat before everyone is ready, and if so, you may begin when a few of the other guests are ready. But how many people have learned to pace themselves? Have you ever looked around when you have finished eating to find that the rest of the party still has half their dinner left to consume? Or even worse, have you had to gobble your meal at the last minute when you realized that everyone else was ready for dessert?

Our first president tackles this pacing question himself in Rule

103: *In Company of your Betters be not longer in eating than they are.* Of course, in modern times we think of our fellow diners as equals, not as betters or inferiors; but the gist of George's message holds up: keep pace with the others at the table.

If you must leave the table before the meal is completed, ask to be excused. Otherwise, wait until everyone has finished eating. Before rising from the table, remember to thank the person who provided the meal. If you can honestly compliment the food, and sometimes even if you cannot, do so. In bountiful America, it is easy to take food for granted and forget to appreciate every meal as a gift and a blessing.

FINAL THOUGHTS

When we share food with genuine good manners—being considerate of the food, the place, and each other—it makes life more pleasant. If we cling so tightly to the rules that they override our sense of humor and inhibit our gusto for the aromas, beauty, and textures of good food, we can miss the point of simply enjoying a fine meal with people we like. Sometimes, in the right time and place, we get the most pleasure while eating with family and friends when we bend the rules. Is not a summer barbecue made better when we pick up ribs dripping with juicy flavor or corn on the cob oozing with butter? The very best manners are perfected by a little sauce. Even George would not have a rule against that.

CHAPTER EIGHT

Out And About

Being to advise or reprehend any one, consider whether it ought to be in publick or in Private; presently, or at Some other time in what terms to do it & in reproving Shew no Sign of Cholar but do it with all Sweetness and Mildness.

—Rule 45

If as written in our Declaration of Independence we do "hold it to be a self-evident truth that all men are created equal," why are we not nicer to one another? Why do we fail to consider the impact of our actions on others? What happened to the atmosphere of respect and consideration? Do we still care about the well-being of anybody but ourselves? Can we be helpful and cooperative? Where is our spirit of community?

George Washington was well aware of the effort it took to balance freedom of expression and civility. *Sleep not when others Speak, Sit not when others stand, Speak not when you Should hold your Peace, walk not on when others Stop*, he tells us in Rule 6. Fit in, not in a bid for blind conformity, but in the interests of promoting peace and goodwill.

Around Town

Whether we live in an urban, suburban, or country setting; whether we rent or own; whether we dwell in a townhouse, subdivision, or farm, we all have neighbors. We all want good neighbors, and we know that one key necessity is being good neighbors ourselves. Through interaction, the barriers between people gradually crumble, a sense of belonging emerges, and a community thrives. In small towns, where we may actually encounter people we know, polite behavior comes naturally. The bigger our environment and the more strangers we deal with, the more anonymous we feel and the lower our standards of behavior can become.

Among Crowds

Americans are independent. We like the freedom of wide-open spaces and, as a result, standing in line or moving in crowds is difficult for us. But alas, crowds are a fact of life. We must wait our turn at the post office, the stadium, and even in a concessions line.

On the sidewalks of busy cities, we can feel as if we are drowning in an ocean of humanity. Each step is a challenge as we try to zigzag around the pet walker, pass the throngs of tourists, and dodge the energetic young skateboarders. Sometimes, amazing as it may be, we ourselves get in the way of others— *that* we can do something about. Are you taking up more than your fair share of space? Practice awareness so that you do not inadvertently hinder the normal flow of the crowd. Stay to the right, walk no more than two abreast, and change to single file when others need to pass.

One of the simplest gestures of goodwill is standing back to allow a fellow citizen to go through a door first. After President Adams and Vice President Jefferson's inauguration, Washington insisted that they exit the chamber before him. Because doormen are no longer readily available, either hold the door as the other party enters first, or hold it for the party behind you. Never pretend you do not see an approaching person and allow the door to slam in his or her face. If you are the recipient of the courtesy, always acknowledge the thoughtfulness of the one holding the door. If you are in a party with several people, do not burst through *en masse* while the poor door-holder waits. After a few of you have gone through, step aside and hold the door yourself.

Are you oblivious? Do you inadvertently block others by standing in front of an entranceway or at the bottom of an escalator? Pay attention to the people trying to get past you. Have you been reprimanded for breaking into a line when there was no apparent line? Before you rush to the counter, look around and confirm that others were not waiting first.

Follow someone around a town, and you will learn a lot about his character. Notice how he treats the merchandise, the clerks, and the other customers, and you will discover his "real" personality.

We all know the shopper who, with a stunning sense of entitlement, wreaks havoc with the merchandise. In the clothing store, he rummages through the carefully displayed sweaters. After trying on seven pairs of pants, he drops them on the dressing room floor and leaves the store without a word. In the grocery store, he changes his mind about the purchase of a frozen food selection and leaves it to melt in the chip aisle. He could have handed the unwanted item to the cashier, but why should he bother? He has no concern for the waste, mess, and health hazard he has left behind.

The aisle and shelf blocker does not notice (or perhaps does not care) that his immobile cart is preventing other shoppers from getting by or accessing a certain shelf. In the parking lot, he neglects to return the cart to the cart return. At best, the unattended cart takes up parking space; at worst, it rolls and dents another car.

The rude shopper finds power (he usually feels powerless in every other aspect of his life) by regarding service personnel as his inferiors. The polite shopper treats all employees—no matter their job description—with courtesy. Our Founding Father tells us the same in Rule 67: *Detract not from others neither be excessive in Commanding.* You are not impressing anyone by ordering clerks and counter help around today any more than you would have two centuries ago.

When Washington opened an account with an English merchant to purchase clothing and other luxury goods, he wrote a warm note: "I should be glad to cultivate the most intimate correspondence with you."[1] Unfortunately, Washington's love of finery occasionally exceeded his ability to pay, and the correspondence became less friendly. When Washington was notified of his debt and asked for payment, his courtesy failed him, and he responded with outrage: "Reason and prudence naturally dictates to every man of common sense the thing that is right, and you might have rest assured that so fast as I could make the remittances without distressing myself too much, my inclinations would have prompted me to it."[2]

The millions of people who work in customer service jobs face a tide of customer rudeness every day. The clerk greets you with "How are you today?" "May I help you?" or "Did you find everything you were looking for?" Only too often, his or her politeness is not reciprocated. (Go to the self-checkout lane if you cannot give the attendant the same undivided attention you want him to give to your purchases.) Finish you cell phone conversation before you approach the register and be nice. Yes, you may be frustrated by the line, the prices, or the merchandise selection, but do not take out your anger on the hapless cashier.

As you conclude your sales transaction, dignify the exchange by placing the money or credit card in the cashier's hand. Have you ever seen someone cavalierly toss the payment across the counter? Does he think his station in life is so far above the cashier's that the slightest inadvertent physical contact would be loathsome?

ON THE ROAD

When giving instructions for a new carriage, George Washington wanted the best. He suggested that it be painted jade green and gold and that "any other Ornaments as may not have a heavy and tawdry look together with my Arms agreeable to the impression here sent [should] be added by way of decoration. . . . On the harness let my Crest be engraved."[3] If he had lived in the age of the automobile, would the Washington seal and coat of arms have been emblazoned on a custom paint job?

As George loved his carriage, we love our cars. Sleek, shiny, and fast, the car embodies all that we fantasize about and covet: freedom, beauty, and power. Unfortunately, the automobile, which used to make our spirits soar with a sense of freedom and mobility, is becoming shackled by higher and higher gasoline prices, congestion in the cities, and crowding on the highways. We need to gather our wits to keep from making ourselves and our fellow travelers miserable and from letting frustration drive us over the edge into dangerous behavior.

TRAFFIC CONGESTION

"Damn, damn this traffic jam, how I hate to be late" is a universal lament put into song by James Taylor. Traffic jams do not discriminate. They threaten to materialize whenever more than two cars share the road.

That mass of cars you can see as you approach from a distance is a multi-lane traffic jam. The courteous driver accepts the inevitable bottleneck of road repairs and wrecks, grits his teeth, and patiently waits his turn. The rude driver beats on the steering wheel, eyes the emergency lane, eases into said lane, zooms past the backed-up cars, thrusts his fender back into the traffic, and nudges his car to the front of the line.

The two-lane road traffic jam is the snail-paced procession forming behind the repetitively stopping school bus, garbage truck, mailman, slow-moving tractor, or lost driver. The safe driver looks for the opportunity of a curve-free, flat road before passing. The dangerous driver ignores those double-line warnings, pushes the pedal to the metal, tailgates, and then roars past the offending vehicle and breezes on down the road. Does he ever look back to the wake of vehicles he has endangered or possibly even forced into the ditch?

If you can pass safely, do so. If passing is impossible and alternate routes are unavailable, you might just have to accept that the slow car is actually abiding by the speed limit. Even if the offending car is traveling *below* the speed limit, trying to alert the slow poke by tailgating and blinking your headlights is more likely to cause a wreck than to accelerate his pace. If all else fails, switch to decaf, enjoy your music, and breathe deeply.

For an attitude adjustment, compare the interstate highways of today with the primitive roads of colonial America. On his tour of the northern states, Washington complained, "The Massachusetts roads are amazingly crooked to suit the convenience of every man's fields, and the directions you receive from the people equally blind and ignorant."[4] George Washington took eight days to go from Mount Vernon to New York for his inauguration as the first president of the United States.

We all think we are the victims of traffic jams and rarely realize it when we are the source of the problem. Looking for an address, fiddling with an electronic device, handing drinks to another passenger—there are many legitimate reasons to go slow, but check your rear-view mirror. If you see a long line of cars behind you, you might be causing congestion. Move to the right if there is more than one lane. Otherwise, increase your speed or pull over to allow the other vehicles to pass you. Whether you are at the bank or a fast-food outlet, pull away from the drive-through window after you have checked your money or food but before you organize your checkbook or put a straw in your beverage. Go with the flow.

Cooperation

Exquisite timing is the mark of a smooth driver. Jackrabbit starts and unnecessary braking jerk around your passengers and alarm other drivers. Neither proving the speed of a fast car nor displaying the remaining power in a rattletrap entitles you to zoom fifty miles per hour in a twenty-five miles per hour zone or to weave in and out of traffic to get ahead.

If you are going to change lanes or make a turn, use your blinker, and do it in advance of making your move. It just takes a quick flick of the wrist to communicate your intent to fellow drivers, and it is the law. Usually the blinker disengages with a turn of the wheel, but be aware that you might need another simple flick to "off" to avoid blinking confusingly for miles down the road.

Take note: there really are many nice people who help you change lanes or enter the flow of traffic. Show appreciation with a short wave of thanks. This gesture indicates your recognition of their thoughtfulness and reinforces for you and the other drivers a certain fellowship and cooperation on the roadway. Appreciation of kindness begets more kindness and more safety on the road for everyone. Contrarily, road rage—obscene hand gestures, aggressive horn usage, and maniacal screaming—can escalate to dangerous street fights.

Carpools

The benefits of carpooling are many—you can save gas, lessen wear and tear on the automobile, reduce traffic congestion, and maybe even enjoy some companionship. To work well, carpooling requires coordination, cooperation, and flexibility from participants.

When you are the driver, be on time and welcome your passenger to a clutter-free seat. Instead of a last-minute tossing of shopping bags, food containers, or mail, prepare a space for your guest before he opens the car door.

When you are the passenger, be ready to leave at the designated time and keep an eye out for your ride. Ask permission before entering the car with latte and sticky bun in hand. A bump in the road, abrupt braking, or a sharp curve, and your drink and snack are splattered all over the car's interior.

A pleasant passenger is not a backseat driver. Unless danger is impending, it is not necessary to announce when the light signals change, when to switch lanes, or when other cars are braking or speeding. Skip the dramatic gestures—gasping and pushing your foot on an imaginary brake accomplish nothing.

As adults, we have matured beyond our days of racing a sibling to the car and yelling "shotgun," yet the sense of mild disgrace lingers when we are banished to the back seat. If you are one of multiple passengers and find yourself in the coveted "shotgun" seat, voluntarily rotate front and back seat positions so everyone has a chance to hold the front seat.

BICYCLES

The mix of cars and bicycles is an uneasy one. The motorist views the bicyclist as yet another obstacle to negotiate; the cyclist fears the motorist will kill him. The motorist is in a hurry; the cyclist accepts a slower pace. The motorist wears the car frame as a suit of armor; the cyclist wears only a helmet. The motorist prefers controlled air conditioning; the bicyclist enjoys the fresh breeze in his face. With all these differences, no wonder there is a driver-versus-rider hostility as four-wheelers and two-wheelers compete for the same limited road.

Both parties need to avoid distractions and be fully aware

of their surroundings. The big guy (automobile) compromises everyone's safety if he is blasting music and/or texting, but the little guy (bicyclist) should remember that he is not a ten-year-old playing in some suburban cul-de-sac and that those dual earphones block the warning sounds of approaching cars or pedestrians. Once the cyclist hits the road, the rules of the road take effect: ride with the traffic and not against it, obey stop signs, use hand signals, and, like any slow-moving vehicle, allow speedier vehicles to pass.

FINAL THOUGHTS

The litany of our misdemeanors is long. Why so many breaches of decorum? Are we experiencing a coarsening of culture? Well, maybe a little, but most of the rudeness we experience or dish out is the inadvertent product of the increasing pace of our lives. We think we are not being productive if we are not simultaneously moving, talking, texting, and reading. Insular in attitude— unaware of ordinary things and everyday practices—we fail to be cognizant of our surroundings.

The chronicles of our daily lives reveal the most about us. What is your public face? As you drive around, go to appointments, or stroll the shops, are you set for battle or cooperation? Do you return home exhausted from your confrontations, or are you energized by the conviviality of the crowd? When you are out and about, whether you know the people around you or not, you will be recognized for who you are. A jerk will be seen as a jerk wherever he or she goes. A nice person generally will receive the same courtesies he or she extends to others. A polite and thoughtful neighbor or traveler will find himself surrounded, almost miraculously, by friendly smiles and welcome voices— both in the smallest hamlets and in the largest capitals of the world.

CHAPTER NINE

Human Frailty

Reproach none for the Infirmities of Nature, nor Delight to Put them that have in mind thereof.

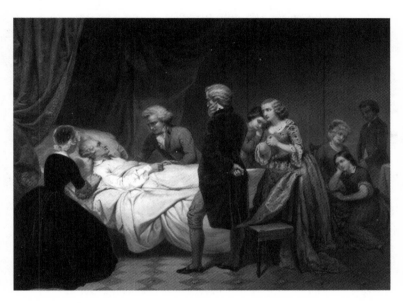

Life is messy, and physical frailty is one of the bumps in the road. We have a great need to maintain the illusion that we and those we love are immortal, but inevitably somewhere along the line, the ravages of time—accidents, sickness, or (heaven forbid) death—lie in wait. No wonder wedding vows demand "for better, for worse, for richer, for poorer, in sickness or in health, to love and to cherish 'til death us do part." Heart disease, cancer, and infection do not discriminate. Accidents are random. Everyone is vulnerable. No one is immune. As humans, we must grapple with the effects of aging, disease, decline, and death.

These days, the weak are so often whisked away to rehab facilities and the aged to retirement communities that dealing with illness, disability, and death has become awkward. The fear of saying or doing the wrong thing often keeps people from doing anything at all, but it need not be so uncomfortable. We need to abolish all stigmas associated with frailty and remember that most illnesses are not contagious.

Treat the infirm as you would treat any friend. Be tender with the young, compassionate with the aged, and tolerant of the weak. The best way to give solace is simply to be there with your time, thoughtfulness, and understanding.

ILLNESS

In visiting the Sick, do not Presently play the Physician if you be not Knowing therein.

—Rule 38

George Washington was well acquainted with sickness. By age twenty-five, he had survived small pox, pleurisy, malaria, and dysentery. Relying on his strong constitution to get well, George Washington rejected unsolicited medical advice: *"You know I never take anything for a cold. Let it go as it came."*[1] His preferred remedy for a sore throat was a syrup of vinegar, molasses, and butter.

Like George, most sick people hope they will get better by themselves. Unfortunately, they often do not, and then we need and want to help them. Washington knew better than to play doctor, but we too often have not learned that lesson. It seems today that everybody is an expert on whatever ails you. If you have a cold, Granny's concoction of lemon and honey is the solution. For aching joints, here is the perfect homeopathic remedy. When you suffer stomach pain, it might just be in your head. Of course we are only trying to help, but we should leave the task of dispensing prescriptions to the doctor.

A lot of phony medical advice comes from sheer awkwardness. How should we talk to the sick? Our Founding Father confronted this problem, too. In Rule 43, he tells us, *Do not express Joy before one sick or in pain for that contrary Passion will aggravate his Misery*. Now, he is not telling us to keep our conversation gloomy. He just means you should not ramble on about how much fun you are going to have next week at the Super Bowl when you visit your friend just starting radiation and chemotherapy.

This is good advice, and we can add to it. Discouraging words are clearly out of place in a sickroom, as are any actions that interfere with the effort to get well or that add to the burden of sickness. Piously clucking, "If only you had not smoked and drank so much, or maybe if you had exercised more," puts the onus of guilt on the patient for what has befallen him. What purpose does such a lambasting serve?

It is better not to ask someone how he first discovered his disease. You may without realizing it be implying, "I'm scared to death that I might have what you have. Tell me so that I can discover it early before I become as sick as you." For transmittable diseases, asking how he got it might imply that you are accusing him or that you are worried he might pass it on to you.

If the patient has very recently had surgery, a bad fall, or a vomiting episode, do not ask, "How are you feeling today?" Our culture of induced good cheer requires the response "Fine, thank you," and your sick friend is not feeling fine, thank you. In fact, she is probably writhing in pain.

Expressing pity by taking the attitude, "You are sick, I am well, and may I never get what you have" or, even worse, "I have nothing in common with the dying and do not know what to say," has more to do with your state of mind than that of the patient. A moribund sympathy is not helpful.

We have all attempted to cheer a patient with upbeat affirmations, such as "I know you will feel better soon," "If anyone can beat it, it's you," or "You gotta think positive." Bad moves all. Your intentions may be good, but because you do not know the medical prognosis, such optimism is often false. It can also be downright irritating. Please—skip the exhortations to be brave and happy. When you are ill, there is nothing worse than having someone sashay in and say, "Let's turn that frown upside down." The patient, crotchety as he may be, is working hard enough to get well and does not need undue pressure from you. Pain, anger, or depression may be part of the healing cycle.

What, then, is left to say? Sit and listen. Let the patient share tales of woe, memories of good times, or hopes for the future. If she is not responsive to your efforts, allow her some behavioral latitude and do not take it personally. Healing requires great energy, and the patient might well be exhausted. Take the cue in conversation from the person who is sick. Some people want to discuss their prognosis and detail their treatment step by step. Others prefer to behave outwardly as if nothing is wrong. It may help to remember that what is needed from you, much more than conversation, is simple faithfulness and companionship. Illness is similar to a journey with constantly changing destinations; a good friend stays the course wherever it might lead.

There are often practical ways to be of assistance. If someone is housebound, bring a meal, run some errands, or perform some household chores. Call, visit, or send a note or flowers. Any gesture of goodwill will be appreciated. Just do something.

Practice loyalty to those who are in your service. The accountant may have cancer; the lawyer may suffer a heart attack; the housekeeper may break a leg. Do not, as the expression goes, "kick them when they are down." Temporary provisions can always be made until the person is able to return to work or other arrangements become necessary.

DEATH

We will die, that much is certain, and everyone we have ever loved and cared about will die too, sometimes heartbreakingly before us. In the West, through Victorian times, mortality was discussed openly. Death was the "final curtain"—the unmovable fact—and there were elaborate rituals to bridge the joy of life and the sorrow of death.

Modern society has a tendency to tiptoe around death, and both sacred and mundane rituals have become fuzzy. How do we get the dead and living where they each need to be? Should visitation take place the day before or the day of the service? In the family home or the funeral parlor? Did the deceased leave a last will and testament? Is the body to be cremated or embalmed? If the choice is cremation, should the ashes be displayed prominently at the memorial and where should they finally go? If the body is to be buried, should the casket be open or closed? Should the service be held at the grave or in a church? Whatever the choice, rituals and ceremonies exist to comfort the living and honor the dead. Unfortunately, for many of us, these ceremonies can be uncomfortable.

FUNERAL DEMEANOR

Superflous Complements and All Affectation of Ceremonie are to be avoided, yet when due they are not to be Neglected.
—Rule 25

Though funerals and memorials are termed "celebrations of

life," these services remain a solemn and subdued recognition of the passing of a life. Dress with dignity. Black is not a requirement, but wear clothes that are conservative in style and somber in color, such as gray, beige, brown, or navy.

EXPRESSING SYMPATHY

You should not outdo the immediate family in the passion of your grief, nor should you try to be the life of the party. As death is an emotional event and guidelines are few, it is often difficult to know what to say. Whatever you do say, make it a sincere expression of your concern and affection. If you are not personally acquainted with the family, introduce yourself, say how you knew the deceased, and extend a brief condolence.

Gossip is to be avoided entirely. No questions should be raised about the cause of death or the size of the inheritance. Honor any confidential information you may possess. It is not fair to speak unkindly about the deceased, as, needless to say, he does not have the opportunity to defend himself. George Washington probably refers more to the quick than to the dead in Rule 89, but it still applies: *Speak not Evil of the absent for it is unjust.*

If you cannot get the words out—and even if you can—convey your sympathy in writing. A condolence note may be brief. Express your sympathy with an "I am so sad," "Sorry," or "Please accept my deepest condolences." Refer to the dead by name and recall a memory or a special quality of the deceased. End the letter with a thoughtful word or hope: "My love is with you always," or "You are in my thoughts and prayers." However, to avoid a "canned" closing, stick to language you would use in normal conversation.

Friends and family members are increasingly being given the opportunity to voice a remembrance of the deceased. Before you open your mouth, however, be mindful that a eulogy is a statement sanctifying the life of the deceased. Seek to capture the essence of the dead—even the lovable quirks. If you are unsure about whether a tale you are about to tell is too honest or revealing, it probably is. Likewise, take care not to digress into stories that say more about you than the deceased. When there is to be more than one eulogy, keep yours short, no more than five minutes.

Grieving does not end with the burial. The bereft are sad for a long period of time, and often their loneliness is exacerbated by people avoiding them for fear of not knowing what to say. Continue to support the grieving by keeping in touch. Do not push, but give them a chance to share memories or maybe even indulge in a little nostalgia. Include the widow or widower in your social plans and greet them at all events.

Be careful that your attention to the family of the deceased is social and sincere. Stockbrokers and real estate agents should not rush to the vulnerable heirs with the motive of making a distress sale. It is often difficult for the grieving to make reasonable business decisions. Answer questions, do research, and, above all else, give them time.

WHEN THE LOSS IS YOURS

As a result of today's sophisticated medical procedures, dying is often a long process; and by the time it is over, the living are overwhelmed. If you are a member of a family facing an inevitable death, you are also facing these modern issues. There is no shame in preparing ahead of time for the beloved's demise—giving special consideration to your exhausted state and making allowances for today's complex family situations.

Keep in mind that it is not *all* up to you. Listen to the wishes of the dying–they may remember things that in your distress you have forgotten. On his deathbed, George Washington was characteristically competent and precise, directing his secretary, Tobias Lear, "Do you arrange and record all my late military letters and papers. Do you arrange my accounts and settle my books . . . and let Rawlins finish recording my other letters which he has begun."[2]

If the end is imminent, stop denying and start planning the memorial or funeral. It may seem morbid, but this is the final tribute to a special person in your life. Think about the best music, scripture, and flowers. Write a rough draft of the obituary. Let those who are to speak have a chance to prepare remarks. If there is to be a reception, plan the food and beverages.

Modern families are full of ex-spouses, stepchildren, and former in-laws. Modern careers are usually serial, leaving behind a variety of ex-partners, ex-bosses, and ex-colleagues. Even if you do not like someone, bury the hatchet and let bygones be bygones. Death is not the time to be vindictive. Welcome the wayward brother or repentant business partner. Because the present spouse makes the burial decisions and sits in the prominent position, she or he can afford to be gracious to the ex-spouse.

Since grief can cloud one's judgment, it is even more important when responding to visitors' condolences at a memorial or funeral to keep conversation simple. Limit your comments to "Thank you for coming." If you know you are going to choke, just clasp your hands and let your sad expression do the talking for you.

Even in bereavement, it is important to say thank you for condolence notes, food, flowers, and *in memoriam* donations. A printed card is simplest: "The family of _____ deeply appreciates and gratefully acknowledges your kind expression of sympathy." To make it more personal, sign the card or insert a handwritten note such as, "Your thoughtful concern brought much comfort during this most difficult time. A heart full of thanks."

Honoring the Dead

Like rituals, commemorative symbols and epitaphs can be an outward and visible sign of an inward and spiritual grace. They may play an important part in healing the pain of the loss of a loved one.

If erecting a roadside cross alleviates your grief and is allowed in your community, do it. However, either take it down after a period of time or maintain it with love. A leaning cross choked with weeds and surrounded by faded and dirty plastic flowers is no honor to the dead. In the long run, a plaque might prove a better and more permanent tribute.

Upon his mother Mary's death, George Washington embraced appropriate decorative symbols. He ordered black cockades (ribbons) for his household staff, and he wore badges of mourning for at least five months. Ironically, Washington never marked his mother's grave. There was no gravestone for her until three decades after the president's death.

If you are charged with composing the obituary, you have a major responsibility. By all means, make it personal, but remember that this is a public announcement. Will the reader understand pet nicknames or the often convoluted intricacies of today's complex and blended family ties? There is no need to try to cover everything or go in for lengthy eloquence. The length of an obituary is by no means the measure of the success of someone's life. Be succinct—state where the deceased was born and educated, what important things he did for the community, by whom he is survived, and where remembrances are to be sent. To avoid hurt feelings or later disagreements, have other family members approve the final version.

Technology has expanded the obituary options beyond the traditional newsprint. Friends and families can now opt for everything from online guest books to video presentations. Use these new tools if you find comfort in them, but try not to go overboard. Again, let others advise; grief may cloud otherwise good judgment.

Martha Washington wanted to hold and share physical evidence of her belated husband. After his death, she distributed locks of his hair. Give a memento of the deceased to relatives and friends—anyone will treasure a book, picture, piece of china, silver, or crystal that belonged to someone they held dear.

Honor the person who has died, but more importantly, be there for those left behind. Let the living know how much you care by treating everyone every day as if there were no tomorrow.

Final Thoughts

Human frailty can render one selfish, defensive, and miserable; or it can translate to an acceptance of the vicissitudes of life as well as an increased sensitivity to others. Facing sickness, disability, and death with equanimity and acceptance is easier said than done. On his deathbed, Washington told his three doctors, "I feel myself going. I thank you for your attention. You had better not take any more trouble about me; but let me go off quietly: I cannot last long."[3] His last words were "Tis well."[4]

CHAPTER TEN

The Next Generation

Honour & Obey your Natural Parents altho they be Poor.

—Rule 108

George Washington left a challenge for us to tell the truth, keep our word, and look after the interests of others. He asserted, "It should be the highest ambition of every American to extend his views beyond himself and to bear in mind that his conduct will not only affect himself, his country, and his immediate posterity; but that its influence may be co-extensive with the world and stamp political happiness or misery on ages yet unborn."[1]

How does one positively affect posterity? The awesome task of child-rearing is one filled with questions. What tools are required for proper human interaction? How does one successfully align the child's special attributes with the needs and wants of society? How does one teach the art of consideration? How is a child to tackle the intricacies of right and wrong or the necessary back and forth of dealing with others? How does one guide a child to know when to stand up for his rights and when to practice restraint?

Answering these questions one by one is daunting and maybe impossible. It is better here to start with first principles. We need, quite simply, to instill in youth the desire to make the world a better place and the understanding that this can only happen when they give of themselves. We need to promote their daily practice, in small things as in large, of telling the truth, respecting the feelings of others, choosing kind words, and performing thoughtful acts.

Helicopter Parenting

The bird builds a nest, sits on its eggs, and feeds its fledglings. When the time is right, a push from the nest, a quick lesson in flight, and a short course in foraging, ready the young bird to "wing it" on his own. Due to the complexities of human existence, we cannot, like birds, one day simply declare, "You're grown up," and push our offspring out of our lives. Humans have a much longer period of childhood dependency than any other creature on the planet—and it takes every year of it to prepare the next generation to assume its place at the head of the planet's food chain. If our progeny are to thrive on their own, we must first create a secure space from which they are able to venture out and bravely encounter uncertainty.

Conscientious adults often skew the precise mixture of "testing your wings" and "keeping you safe" necessary to get a child to adulthood intact and functioning. Sometimes, thinking a safe environment is a place without risk, doting parents, grandparents, aunts and uncles, and even teachers, preachers, friends, and neighbors suffocate the child in an attempt to keep him safe. Often we do not know how to play our hand—when to intervene and when to let kids suffer the consequences of their actions. We are soft when we should be hard and hard when we should be yielding. We may teach our children tenderness but forget to teach them resilience, or we may tell them to be tough but forget to tell them to be kind.

Martha Washington was the original helicopter parent. She found it difficult to travel with her husband unless both children came along. When away from her children, she anxiously imagined that a knock on the door or the bark of a dog was news of sickness or accident.

In real life, benign parents will not always be able to stand guard (if only fairy godmothers offered a convenient replacement!). The cavalry will not arrive to save the day, and Prince Charming will not glide in to kiss our darling and wake her from a bad dream. We just have to accept this, and so do our kids. A coddled and overly indulged child, having never solved a problem for himself, been denied immediate gratification, or been forced to practice self-control, becomes lost in the maze of daily living. Incapacitated by a lack of adaptive skills, he becomes easily confused and agitated. He does not know when to compete and when to cooperate.

Teach Your Children Well

Telling a doting parent to impose a firmer discipline on his or her child can be difficult. Here even Washington failed. He found his stepson, Jacky Custis, an indolent, self-indulgent young man who loved only horses, girls, and the finer things of life. When Martha did not support his efforts to improve the young man, Washington, the most powerful man in the country, backed off, afraid to cross his wife on the loaded subject of how to raise her children.

An ungoverned child does little to ingratiate himself anywhere with anybody. Without boundaries in place, children's natural combination of energy and curiosity can be invasive and even destructive. The lessons of life that children often absorb through a smear of tears and tantrums need to be both cushioned by adult tenderness but also reinforced by adult firmness. With a strong emotional connection in place, parents can hold children in esteem and still hold them accountable.

Much in our contemporary culture seems to militate against the well-established, time-honored rules of conduct that promote human connection and rapport. Many of the celebrity role models for the young seem to revel in the flagrant disregard of these codes, and the media in turn revels in the celebrities' bad behavior, thereby offering them even more fame. Being bad thus seems to pay off, at least in the moment-to-moment world inhabited by the young. It is the task of adults to provide a larger perspective and insist that in the long run and in real life (not the tabloid world where rock stars and top athletes live), courtesy wins.

HEART

It is natural for a child to be inwardly focused and assume he is the center of the world; but as soon as a child is able to say, "You hurt my feelings," he can begin to respect the feelings of others and show that respect in simple ways of sharing and caring. It is not hard to learn that friendship means "lending a hand" rather than "pushing and shoving" and "taking turns" rather than screaming "me first."

Prepare your child to be of service in the community. Once a young person gets the spirit of volunteerism, the rewards will keep him giving for life. For a child, "doing good" can be as simple as putting some of his allowance in the Salvation Army bucket or setting up a lemonade stand to raise money for a worthy cause. Set a good example yourself. Altruism, like the apple of the proverb, does not fall far from the tree. Youngsters emulate acts of empathy and generosity; so take your child with you to deliver that casserole to the new mother or sick friend. Participate as a family in a charitable fundraising "walkathon" or "fun run." Develop that charitable bent, because generosity can be habit forming.

Bullying (taunting, spreading rumors, excluding others from activities, or physically abusing) has always existed, but now that technology has given the bully more weapons, the problem is growing worse. The Internet, Facebook, and phone cameras have given children powerful tools before they have developed the moral compass they need to handle them. Do not let your own kids be bullies–establish a zero tolerance policy for meanness. Likewise, a child should know that mocking, staring, or pointing at a person who is handicapped, foreign, or just different is mean, and let them know that you wholly disapprove of it. Washington backs you with Rule 71: *Gaze not on the marks and blemishes of Others and ask not how they came.*

FORM

Legend has it that George Washington, our model American, was the perfect child. He respected his elders and never told a lie. And what diligence! No one had to tell him to write a hundred times, "I will not talk in class." He was already busy copying *Rules of Civility & Decent Behaviour in Company and Conversation.* Nathaniel Hawthorne imagined Washington "was born with his clothes on and his hair powdered and made a stately bow on his first appearance in the world." [2] All right, good for George Washington, but let us not draw the wrong conclusion from all this model behavior. Form must not replace substance. Spare us the namby pambies. The rascal Tom Sawyer and the scamp Dennis the Menace are essential to American culture. We need all personalities—the athlete and the scholar, the expressive and the reserved, the messy and the meticulous, the shy and the aggressive. A child may keep his room orderly and wear nice clothes; he may remember to say "yes sir" and to eat with the proper utensils. However, for all these accomplishments, he may be at a loss when it comes to knowing how to get along well with others. Civility is first and foremost a condition of the heart.

Focus on what is *really* important. Good hygiene does not mean sterility. George, a boy who grew up on a farm, certainly experienced his share of dirt. Childhood would not be complete without the delicious feel of mud oozing between the toes or the appreciation of a work of art traced in dust. Allow your children the freedom to get dirty along with the discipline to clean up afterwards. Dirt is not a big deal. Clothes launder, nails come clean, skin can be easily washed. Soap and water is all it takes.

Honesty really is the best policy. Blatant lies, crafty lies, partial lies, meaningless lies, and tactical lies—they are all just lies. The legend of George Washington and the cherry tree teaches the courage it takes to tell the truth. Admitting a mistake earns respect, and a misdeed is usually forgiven more easily than a cover-up. Honesty is also practical—lying only works for a little while; truth usually prevails.

Bragging is always a bad idea. Our first president warns us in Rule 63, *A man ought not to value himself of his Atchievements, or rare Qualities of wit; much less of his riches Virtue or Kindred.* "I am smart, and I can run fast" is the big talk of a show-off. Such cockiness in a young person is offensive. Referring to the wealth and power of one's parents guarantees that peers—and *their* parents—will be put off.

Final Thoughts

A well-honed person is like a work of art. There is something ineluctably enriching and life-enhancing about his aura. We sense his zest for life—that extra special something endowing him with the talent to experience things on a higher plane and with a wider and deeper dimension. A certain mystery to the variety, harmony, and moderation of this young person's style seems to please everyone who has anything to do with him. What adult would not be pleased to participate in developing such a person's particular gifts?

You do not have to be a parent to participate in this. After the death of Martha's son Jacky Custis, Washington informally adopted the deceased's two youngest children. "It has always been my intention, since my expectation of having issue has ceased, to consider the grandchildren of my wife in the same light as I do my own relations." [3] Washington rejoiced especially in his step-granddaughter Nelly, and she acknowledged him in return "with grateful affection as a parent to myself and family." [4]

The mind of a child is fascinating, for it looks at old things with new eyes. Every day, every age, and every rite of passage brings it joys and surprises. In the process of facilitating, protecting, and generally loving our children, we will benefit. The wondrous traits of children—spontaneity, silliness, and frivolity—are all too easily lost in adulthood. While immersing ourselves in the world of our children, we may regain this sense of fun and playfulness, one toy car, doll, and sandcastle at a time. If parenting means teaching children to be adults, it also means teaching adults to be children.

Epilogue

George Washington represents all that is good about the United States of America. Personal integrity, honor, patriotism, and a deeply held sense of duty—he was the whole package rolled into one individual. More than two hundred years after his death, the "Father of our Country" serves as a national icon, an embodiment of many of America's most celebrated ideals.

Lest we get carried away . . . George Washington may have had absolutely lovely manners. He may have known and observed the 110 *Rules of Civility*, but he was not faultless. Behind his mask of calm assuredness, he was human and had human concerns and uncertainties—what could, would, and should he do about his slaves; and how should he, a dutiful son, handle his cantankerous mother? In both cases, George Washington could only turn to conscience and perhaps a little compromise.

George Washington, "liberty's spotless high priest," may have been a hero to his country, but he was no hero to his mother. George needed every ounce of personal discipline and resolve to endure her constant criticism. Mary Ball Washington measured her son's worth by what he could do for her, and apparently he could never do enough. She was outraged that his activities in the French and Indian War and the American Revolution took him out of Virginia and interfered with what she felt were his responsibilities to her. In later years, though he set her up in a house in Fredericksburg and supplied her with money and goods, she complained vociferously and endlessly that she was neglected and in great want. He never did succeed in satisfying her.

Washington's most flagrant failure in modern eyes was his inability to deal forthrightly with the injustice of slavery. Looking back over the arc of history, we find it difficult to understand how the same man who fought for the freedom of our country could own slaves. Though George Washington privately expressed a wish "to liberate a certain species of property which I possess very repugnantly to my feelings,"[1] he did not in fact free his slaves. He stalled. A caveat to his will gave his slaves freedom only after his widow died. Ironically, she freed all the slaves a year after his death.

As society and circumstances change, we seek enlightenment and inspiration from George Washington's example to the nation. It is helpful to use the past to illuminate the present, but change is inevitable, and thank goodness for that. Abandon the bias that yesterday was better than today. Do not hanker after a perceived perfect past when everyone behaved with model decorum and the social waters were never stirred. The challenge for us is to adapt to the modern world while valuing and honoring the traditions of the past. Rather than bemoan the present and long for the good old days or jump feet first into every innovation, we need to consider the implications of our actions as we move forward. Hopefully, we will then be able to preserve the integrity of the past while embracing the best of the future.

On his last day in office, George Washington forecast the many lapses and redemptions of the American experiment. "I trust . . . that the good sense of our countrymen will guard the public weal [sic] against this and every other innovation and that, although we may be a little wrong now and then, we shall return to the right path with more avidity."[2]

Best intentions often go awry. We will never—and can never—be perfect, and we will never—and can never—make other people perfect either. Even with the best plans and careful judgments, things will not always turn out as one hopes. The range of human impulses, enthusiasms, and misperceptions make it impossible to filter out every non-productive and irrational behavior. When the demands of life test the ability to cope, when we feel our control slipping, it is time to pull out our bravery, resilience, and common sense. The ability to act larger than the moment—to let the hard knocks of life propel us to do the right thing no matter how difficult the situation—is the measure of a nation and its people.

In the face of adversity, Americans historically have overcome difficulties with pride and dignity intact. They measure the challenge and deal with it forthrightly and creatively. Remember the perseverance and the "We Can Do It" pluck of GI Joe in overseas battlefields and of Rosie the Riveter in the wartime shipyards. Envision all the little-heralded Americans who consistently demonstrate valor and generosity when faced with catastrophe. In the event of man-made disasters, economic slumps, or the ravages of wildfires and hurricanes, volunteers never fail to step forward and help. In taking heart—that curious mixture of courage and compassion—Americans simply cannot be beat.

We conclude our study of American civility with the same rule George Washington chose to conclude his *Rules of Civility*. It is fittingly a rule that refers to our inner compass. Rule 110 reads, *Labour to keep alive in your Breast that Little Spark of Celestial fire Called Conscience.*

Acknowledgments

SPECIAL THANKS FROM NAN

My immediate family: Husband Gene who can be counted on to support me in any endeavor. Daughters Helen, who continues to be the perfect first child; Lisa, who was born with wisdom and good taste; and Gretchen, who radiates sweetness and all good things. My son Tyllmann who is a gentleman of integrity and moral character. Additional thanks to Andy and Anna who prove the joys of merged families. A special tribute to grandchildren Sam, Mary Jane, Elisabeth, Sloan, Bill, and Charlie. You are my heart. I could not conclude this without recognizing my sons-in-law and the fathers of this next generation. There is Fred (our first reader) who, like George Washington, must have studied at the feet of Seneca; Jim who can match the first president for attention to detail; and Frank whose civility was an inspiration to every page.

My parents, who emphasized the importance of the written word to all seven of their children. Further gratitude to my brothers Mark, for the early encouragement, and John, for the first as well as the final edit.

Savannah couples: Jane and William Moore, Emerson and Mary Ham, Bobby and Margaret Minis, Bobby and Walter Strong, Sam and Gay Inglesby, and Marsha and Perry Brannen. Your patience and feedback on the subject of civility have been invaluable. Friends: Lu Hostetter, Dina Burke, Loretta Wells, Jeanne Armstrong Seals, Helen Marshall, Mimi Harrison Vickers, and Frances Walter. Thanks for sharing new ideas. My grade school best friends forever: writers Summer Brenner and Marticia McKinney. Thanks for your support and guidance. College roommate: Hella Carlson. You are the model for the chapter on correspondence.

The Westminster Schools for good values, Christ Church Savannah for the spirit of brotherly love, and the National Society of Colonial Dames of America for the preservation of American history.

SPECIAL THANKS FROM HELEN

My sons Bill and Charlie, who continue to grow into courteous young gentlemen and make me incredibly proud. My husband

Jim, who embodies all of the character and qualities one could wish for in a partner and is the perfect role model for our children. My mother Nan, who has always put others ahead of herself.

My business partners: Ross Shafer, who makes me laugh every day and whose generous spirit and insightful lessons brighten the lives of those lucky enough to hear him speak. Cam Marston, a true Southern Gentleman who unites the generations. Mark Sanborn, who recognizes that anyone, no matter what his life situation, can achieve the extraordinary. These remarkable men inspire me daily and make my workday fun. In memory of legendary speaker Keith Harrell, who until his last day reminded us all that "Attitude is Everything" and encouraged me not to set this book aside in spite of my work and family duties. Peter Vidmar and Bonnie Blair, two outstanding athletes and people who define "Olympian" in both talent and character. They started out as clients and ended up as friends.

My mother-in-law Jane Broder. My friends Carrie Williamson, Susan Poliquin, Pam Cobb, Amy Thompson, Laney Robinson, Rita Neagli, Pamela Fox and Eleanor Gollob. Professor Ilkka Ronkainen and Dean Ann-Mary Kapusta, who are both long overdue in receiving thanks for the support and encouragement they provided during my memorable years at Georgetown University.

As the final touches were being put on this book, we lost my father-in-law, Al Broder, a wonderful man who was full of love and treated me like his own daughter. When sorting through his possessions, we came across a box of his special memories—including a portrait of George Washington painted when Al was only fourteen years old— about the same age at which Washington copied out the *Rules of Civility*. The coincidence of this discovery was remarkable, but it was not surprising that Washington had been an inspiration to Al.

SPECIAL RECOGNITION
FROM BOTH NAN AND HELEN

Long time and loyal friends: Charlie and Yetty Arp, Bill and Eleanor Effinger, Floyd and Eva Taylor, Jack and Judy Sells, and Tommy and Wally Hills. For over four decades, through thick and thin—you have always been there for us.

Literary agent Mimi Strong, who was the first to believe there was a market for a book on courtesy; Julie Sheehan, who shared her computer skills and enthusiasm; Ann Eckstrom, who cultivated our voice; Kathryn Forgan, who shaped our thoughts; and Betty Darby, who cut the fluff or in literary terms "killed our darlings."Artists Steve Shetsky, for his suggestions, and Ian Doyle, for his clever photoshops. Photographers Chrissy Hall and Robert Cooper for our author pictures. Dawn Bonner for the illustrations from the Mount Vernon Ladies Association collection. Friends Mimi Vickers and Emerson Ham, who patiently proofed the original manuscript. Most important are the team at Pelican Publishing: Nina Kooij and Katy Doll, the editors who acquired and made this book a reality, and Hannah D. Adams and Johanna Rotondo-McCord, the publicists who helped promote it.

Last but not least, we continue to find inspiration in the modern American whose everyday courtesies continue to delight and amaze us.

The Rules Of Civility And Decent Behaviour In Company And Conversation

GEORGE WASHINGTON

The 110 *Rules of Civility* are presented as the teenaged George Washington transcribed them. For the convenience of twenty-first century readers, modern spelling and punctuation are used. A few words have been inserted in brackets for clarity.

1. Every action done in company ought to be with some sign of respect to those that are present.
2. When in company, put not your hands to any part of the body not usually discovered.
3. Show nothing to your friend that may affright him.
4. In the presence of others, sing not to yourself with a humming noise, nor drum with your fingers or feet.
5. If you cough, sneeze, sigh, or yawn, do it not loud but privately; and speak not in your yawning, but put your handkerchief or hand before your face and turn aside.
6. Sleep not when others speak. Sit not when others stand. Speak not when you should hold your peace. Walk not on when others stop.
7. Put not off your clothes in the presence of others, nor go out your chamber half dressed.
8. At play and at fire, it's good manners to give place to the last comer, and affect not to speak louder than ordinary.

9. Spit not in the fire, nor stoop low before it. Neither put your hands into the flames to warm them, nor set your feet upon the fire, especially if there be meat before it.

10. When you sit down, keep your feet firm and even, without putting one on the other or crossing them.

11. Shift not yourself in sight of others, nor gnaw your nails.

12. Shake not the head, feet, or legs. Roll not the eyes, lift not one eyebrow higher than the other. Wry not the mouth, and bedew no man's face with your spittle by approaching too near him when you speak.

13. Kill no vermin, [such] as fleas, lice, ticks, etc. in the sight of others. If you see any filth or thick spittle, put your foot dexterously upon it. If it be upon the clothes of your companions, put it off privately; and if it be upon your own clothes, return thanks to him who puts it off.

14. Turn not your back to others, especially in speaking. Jog not the table or desk on which another reads or writes. Lean not upon anyone.

15. Keep your nails clean and short, also your hands and teeth clean, yet without showing any great concern for them.

16. Do not puff up the cheeks, loll not out the tongue, rub the hands or beard, thrust out the lips, or bite them or keep the lips too open or too close.

17. Be no flatterer, neither play with any that delights not to be played with.

18. Read no letters, books, or papers in company, but when there is a necessity for the doing of it you must ask leave. Come not near the books or writings of another so as to read them unless desired, or give your opinion of them unasked. Also look not nigh when another is writing a letter.

19. Let your countenance be pleasant but in serious matters somewhat grave.

20. The gestures of the body must be suited to the discourse you are upon.

21. Reproach none for the infirmities of nature, nor delight to put them that have in mind thereof.

22. Show not yourself glad at the misfortune of another, though he were your enemy.

23. When you see a crime punished, you may be inwardly pleased; but always show pity to the suffering offender.

24. Do not laugh too loud or too much at any public spectacle.

25. Superfluous compliments and all affectation of ceremony are to be avoided, yet where due they are not to be neglected.

26. In pulling off your hat to persons of distinction, [such] as noblemen, justices, churchmen, etc., make a reverence, bowing more or less according to the custom of the better bred, and quality of the persons. Among your equals, expect not always that they should begin with you first, but to pull off the hat when there is no need is affectation. In the manner of saluting and resaluting in words, keep to the most usual custom.

27. Tis ill manners to bid one more eminent than yourself be covered, as well as not to do it to whom it's due. Likewise, he that makes too much haste to put on his hat, does not well, yet he ought to put it on at the first, or at most second time of being asked. Now what is herein spoken, of qualification in behavior in saluting, ought also be observed in taking of place and sitting down, for ceremonies without bounds are troublesome.

28. If anyone come to speak to you while you are sitting, stand up though he be your inferior. And when you present seats, let it be to everyone according to his degree.

29. When you meet with one of greater quality than yourself, stop, and retire especially if it be at a door or any straight place to give way for him to pass.

30. In walking, the highest place in most countries seems to be on the right hand. Therefore, place yourself on the left of him whom you desire to honor. But if three walk together, the middle place is the most honorable. The wall is usually given to the most worthy if two walk together.

31. If anyone far surpasses others, either in age, estate, or merit, yet would give place to a meaner than himself in his own lodging or elsewhere, the one ought not to accept it. So he on the other part should not use much earnestness nor offer it above once or twice.

32. To one that is your equal, or not much inferior, you are to give the chief place in your lodging. And he to whom it is offered ought at the first to refuse it, but at the second to accept though not without acknowledging his own unworthiness.

33. They that are in dignity or in office have in all places precedence, but while they are young, they ought to respect those that are their equals in birth or other qualities, though they have no public charge.

34. It is good manners to prefer them to whom we speak before ourselves, especially if they be above us, with whom in no sort we ought to begin.

35. Let your discourse with men of business be short and comprehensive.

36. Artificers & persons of low degree ought not to use many ceremonies to Lords, or others of high degree, but respect and highly honor them. Those of high degree ought to treat them with affability and courtesy, without arrogance.

37. In speaking to men of quality, do not lean nor look them full in the face, nor approach too near them. At least keep a full pace from them.

38. In visiting the sick, do not presently play the physician if you be not knowing therein.

39. In writing or speaking, give to every person his due title, according to his degree & the custom of the place.

40. Strive not with your superiors in argument, but always submit your judgment to others with modesty.
41. Undertake not to teach your equal in the art himself professes; it savors of arrogance.
42. Let your ceremonies in courtesy be proper to the dignity of his place with whom you converse. For it is absurd to act the same with a clown and a prince.
43. Do not express joy before one sick or in pain, for that contrary passion will aggravate his misery.
44. When a man does all he can though it succeeds not well, blame not him that did it.
45. Being to advise or reprehend anyone, consider whether it ought to be in public or in private, presently or at some other time, in what terms to do it; & in reproving show no sign of choler but do it with all sweetness and mildness.
46. Take all admonitions thankfully, in what time or place so ever given, but afterwards not being culpable, take a time & place convenient to let him know it that gave them.
47. Mock not nor jest at anything of importance. Break no jests that are sharp biting, and if you deliver anything witty and pleasant, abstain from laughing thereat yourself.
48. Wherein you reprove another, be unblameable yourself, for example is more prevalent than precepts.
49. Use no reproachful language against anyone, neither curse nor revile.
50. Be not hasty to believe flying reports to the disparagement of any.
51. Wear not your clothes foul, ripped or dusty, but see they be brushed once every day at least; and take heed that you approach not to any uncleanness.
52. In your apparel, be modest and endeavor to accommodate nature, rather than to procure admiration. Keep to the fashion of your

equals such as are civil and orderly with respect to times and places.

53. Run not in the streets, neither go too slowly nor with mouth open. Go not shaking your arms, kick not the earth with your feet, go not upon the toes, nor in a dancing fashion.

54. Play not the peacock, looking everywhere about you, to see if you be well decked, if your shoes fit well, if your stockings sit neatly, and clothes handsomely.

55. Eat not in the streets, nor in the house, out of season.

56. Associate yourself with men of good quality if you esteem your own reputation; for 'tis better to be alone than in bad company.

57. In walking up and down in a house only with one in company, if he be greater than yourself, at the first give him the right hand; and stop not till he does; and be not the first that turns, and when you do turn, let it be with your face towards him. If he be a man of great quality, walk not with him cheek by jowl but somewhat behind him, but yet in such a manner that he may easily speak to you.

58. Let your conversation be without malice or envy, for 'tis a sign of a tractable and commendable nature; and in all causes of passion permit reason to govern.

59. Never express anything unbecoming, nor act against the rules moral before your inferiors.

60. Be not immodest in urging your friends to discover a secret.

61. Utter not base and frivolous things among grave and learned men; nor very difficult questions or subjects among the ignorant. Or things hard to be believed. Stuff not your discourse with sentences among your betters nor equals.

62. Speak not of doleful things in a time of mirth or at the table. Speak not of melancholy things [such] as death and wounds, and if others mention them, change if you can the discourse. Tell not your dreams but to your intimate friend.

63. A man ought not to value himself of his achievements or rare qualities of wit, much less of his riches, virtue, or kindred.

64. Break not a jest where none take pleasure in mirth; laugh not aloud nor at all without occasion; deride no man's misfortune though there seem to be some cause.

65. Speak not injurious words neither in jest nor earnest; scoff at none although they give occasion.

66. Be not forward but friendly and courteous. Be the first to salute, hear, and answer; and be not pensive when it's time to converse.

67. Detract not from others, neither be excessive in commending them.

68. Go not thither, where you know not whether you shall be welcome or not. Give not advice without being asked, and when desired do it briefly.

69. If two contend together, take not the part of either unconstrained; and be not obstinate in your own opinion. In things indifferent, be of the major side.

70. Reprehend not the imperfections of others—for that belongs to parents, masters, and superiors.

71. Gaze not on the marks or blemishes of others and ask not how they came. What you may speak in secret to your friend, deliver not before others.

72. Speak not in an unknown tongue in company but in your own language and that as those of quality do and not as the vulgar. Sublime matters treat seriously.

73. Think before you speak. Pronounce not imperfectly, nor bring out your words too hastily but orderly and distinctly.

74. When another speaks, be attentive yourself and disturb not the audience. If any hesitate in his words, help him not nor prompt him without desired; interrupt him not, nor answer him till his speech be ended.

75. In the midst of discourse, ask not of what one treats; but if you perceive

any stop because of your coming, you may well entreat him gently to proceed. If a person of quality comes in while you're conversing, it's handsome to repeat what was said before.

76. While you are talking, point not with your finger at him of whom you discourse, nor approach too near him to whom you talk, especially to his face.

77. Treat with men at fit times about business & whisper not in the company of others.

78. Make no comparisons, and if any of the company be commended for any brave act or virtue, commend not another for the same.

79. Be not apt to relate news if you know not the truth thereof. In discoursing of things you have heard, name not your author. Always a secret discover not.

80. Be not tedious in discourse or in reading unless you find the company pleased therewith.

81. Be not curious to know the affairs of others; neither approach those that speak in private.

82. Undertake not what you cannot perform, but be careful to keep your promise.

83. When you deliver a matter, do it without passion & with discretion, however mean the person you do it to.

84. When your superiors talk to anybody, hearken not thereto and neither speak nor laugh.

85. In company of those of higher quality than yourself, speak not till you are asked a question. Then stand upright, put off your hat and answer in few words.

86. In disputes, be not so desirous to overcome as not to give liberty to each one to deliver his opinion, and submit to the judgment of the major part, especially if they are judges of the dispute.

87. Let your bearing be such as becomes a man grave, settled, and

attentive to that which is spoken, without being too serious. Contradict not at every turn what others say.

88. Be not tedious in discourse; make not many digressions; nor repeat often the same manner of discourse.

89. Speak no evil of the absent, for it is unjust.

90. Being set at meat, scratch not, neither spit, cough nor blow your nose except there's a necessity for it.

91. Make no show of taking great delight in your victuals. Feed not with greediness. Cut your bread with a knife. Lean not on the table; neither find fault with what you eat.

92. Take no salt, or cut bread, when your knife is greasy.

93. Entertaining anyone at table, it is decent to present him with meat. Undertake not to help others undesired by the master or host.

94. If you soak bread in the sauce, let it be no more than what you put in your mouth at a time; and blow not your broth at table, but stay until it cools of itself.

95. Put not your meat to your mouth with your knife in your hand; neither spit forth the stones of any fruit pie upon a dish, nor cast anything under the table.

96. It's unbecoming to stoop much to one's meat. Keep your fingers clean & when foul wipe them on a corner of your table napkin.

97. Put not another bit into your mouth till the former be swallowed. Let not your morsels be too big for the jowls.

98. Drink not, nor talk with your mouth full. Neither gaze about you while you are drinking.

99. Drink not too leisurely nor yet too hastily. Before and after drinking, wipe your lips. Breathe not then or ever with too great a noise, for it is uncivil.

100. Cleanse not your teeth with the tablecloth, napkin, fork or knife; but if others do it, let it be done with a pick tooth [*i.e.*, toothpick].

101. Rinse not your mouth in the presence of others.

102. It is out of use to call upon the company often to eat; nor need you drink to others every time you drink.

103. In company of your betters, be not longer in eating than they are. Lay not your arm, but only your hand, upon the table.

104. It belongs to the chiefest in company to unfold his napkin and fall to meat first; but he ought then to begin in time & to dispatch with dexterity that the slowest may have time allowed him.

105. Be not angry at table, whatever happens; and if you have reason to be so, show it not. Put on a cheerful countenance, especially if there be strangers, for good humor makes one dish of meat a feast.

106. Set not yourself at the upper of the table, but if it be your due or that the master of the house will have it so. Contend not, lest you should trouble the company.

107. If others talk at table, be attentive; but talk not with meat in your mouth.

108. When you speak of God or his attributes, let it be seriously & with words of reverence. Honor & obey your natural parents, although they be poor.

109. Let your recreations be manful, not sinful.

110. Labor to keep alive in your breast that little spark of celestial fire called conscience.

Source Notes

I. Making Time

1. Ron Chernow, *Washington, A Life* (New York: The Penguin Press, 2010), 91.
2. Ibid., 119.
3. Ibid., 353.

II. The Social American

1. Chernow, *Washington*, 88.
2. Ibid., 577.
3. Ibid., 580.
4. James Thomas Flexner, *Washington: The Indispensable Man* (New York: Little Brown and Company, 1974), 7.
5. Chernow, *Washington*, 122.
6. Flexner, *Washington*, 186.

III. Keep in Touch

1. Flexner, *Washington*, 362.
2. Chernow, *Washington*, 395.
3. Ibid., 395.
4. Ibid., 603.
5. Ibid., 605.
6. Ibid., 543.

IV. Free Speech

1. Flexner, *Washington*, 174.
2. Chernow, *Washington*, 604.
3. Ibid., 66.
4. Jared Sparks, *The Writings of George Washington,* vol. 8 (Cambridge: Charles Folsom, printer to the University, 1835), 201.
5. Peter Henriques. "George Washington's Political Philosophy and Personal Opinions." (course, History 615: The Age of George Washington, George Mason University), http://chnm.gmu.edu/courses/henriques/hist615/quotes_by_washington.htm
6. Ibid.
7. Chernow, *Washington*, 363.
8. Ibid., 172.
9. Steven Michael Selzer, *By George, Mr. Washington's Guide to Civility Today* (Kansas City: Andrew McMeel, 2000), 47.
10. ThinkExist.com "Winston Churchill Quotes," thinkexist.com/quotes/winston_churchill/.
11. Paul Leicester Ford, ed., *The Works of Thomas Jefferson in Twelve Volumes,* (New York and London: G. P. Putnam's Sons, 1904) accessed via www.monticello.org/site/research and collections.
12. *Quotations of George Washington* (Belford, MA: Applewood Books, 2003), 7.
13. Richard Brookhiser, *The Rules of Civility* (Charlottesville, VA: University of Virginia Press, 1997), 36.
14. Mark Twain, "A Tramp Abroad " Part 4, www. gutenberg.org/files/119old/orig. 119-h (p.4htm).

V. The Good Sport

1. Chernow, *Washington*, 811.

2. Henry Wiecnek, *An Imperfect God: George Washington, His Slaves and the Creation of America* (New York: Farrar, Straus and Giroux, 2003), 38.

3. *The Guardian*. Web. 26 July, 2004. "What goes around, comes a-round" www.the guardian.com/sport/2004/jul27/cricket.

4. Chernow, *Washington* 588.

VI. Best Foot Forward

1. Chernow, *Washington*, 121.

2. Ibid., 644.

3. Ibid., 429.

4. Wiecnek, *An Imperfect God*, 66.

5. Chernow, *Washington*, 183.

VII. At the Table

1. Flexner, *Washington*, 186.

2. Ibid., 361.

3. Ibid., 186.

4. Chernow, *Washington*, 581.

5. Ibid., 135.

VIII. Out and About

1. Chernow, *Washington*, 64.

2. Flexner, *Washington*, 46.

3. Wiecnek, *An Imperfect God*, 90.

4. Flexner, *Washington*, 229.

IX. Human Frailty

1. Flexner, *Washington*, 397.
2. Ibid., 401.
3. Ibid.
4. Ibid., 402

X. The Next Generation

1. "Washington's Legacy." *George Washington's Mount Vernon.* http://www.mountvernon.org/meet-george-washington/ biography-and-influence/washingtons-legacy. Web. June 14, 2013.
2. Edward G. Lengel, *Inventing George Washington* (New York: Harper Collins, 2011), 38.
3. Chernow, *Washington*, 421.
4. Ibid., 615.

Epilogue

1. Chernow, *Washington*, 709.
2. Ibid., 767.